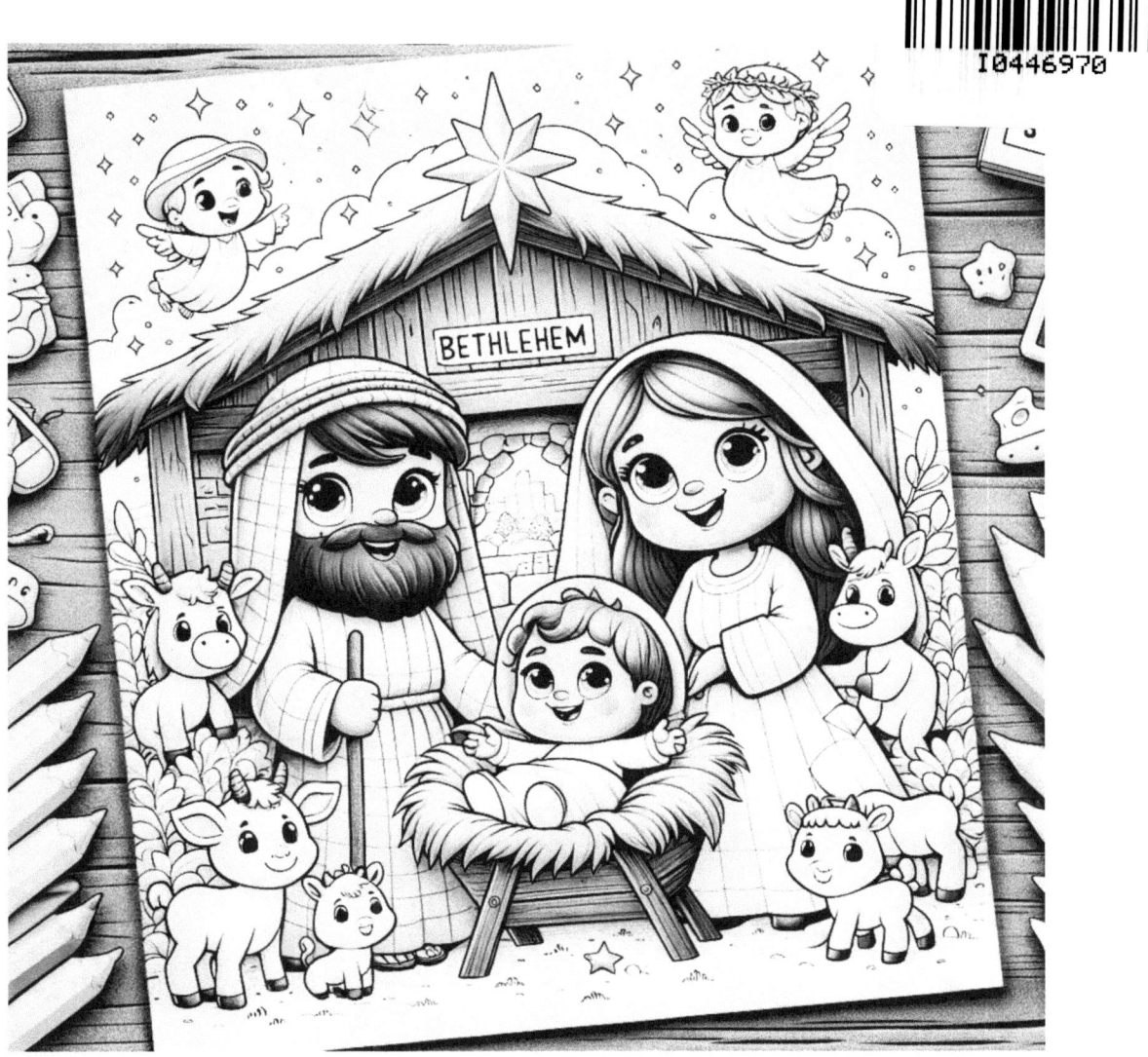

This Book Belongs To:

_____

First Edition
Published in 2023

ISBN
ISBN 9798869718037

Designs by Dale

THE BIRTH OF JESUS

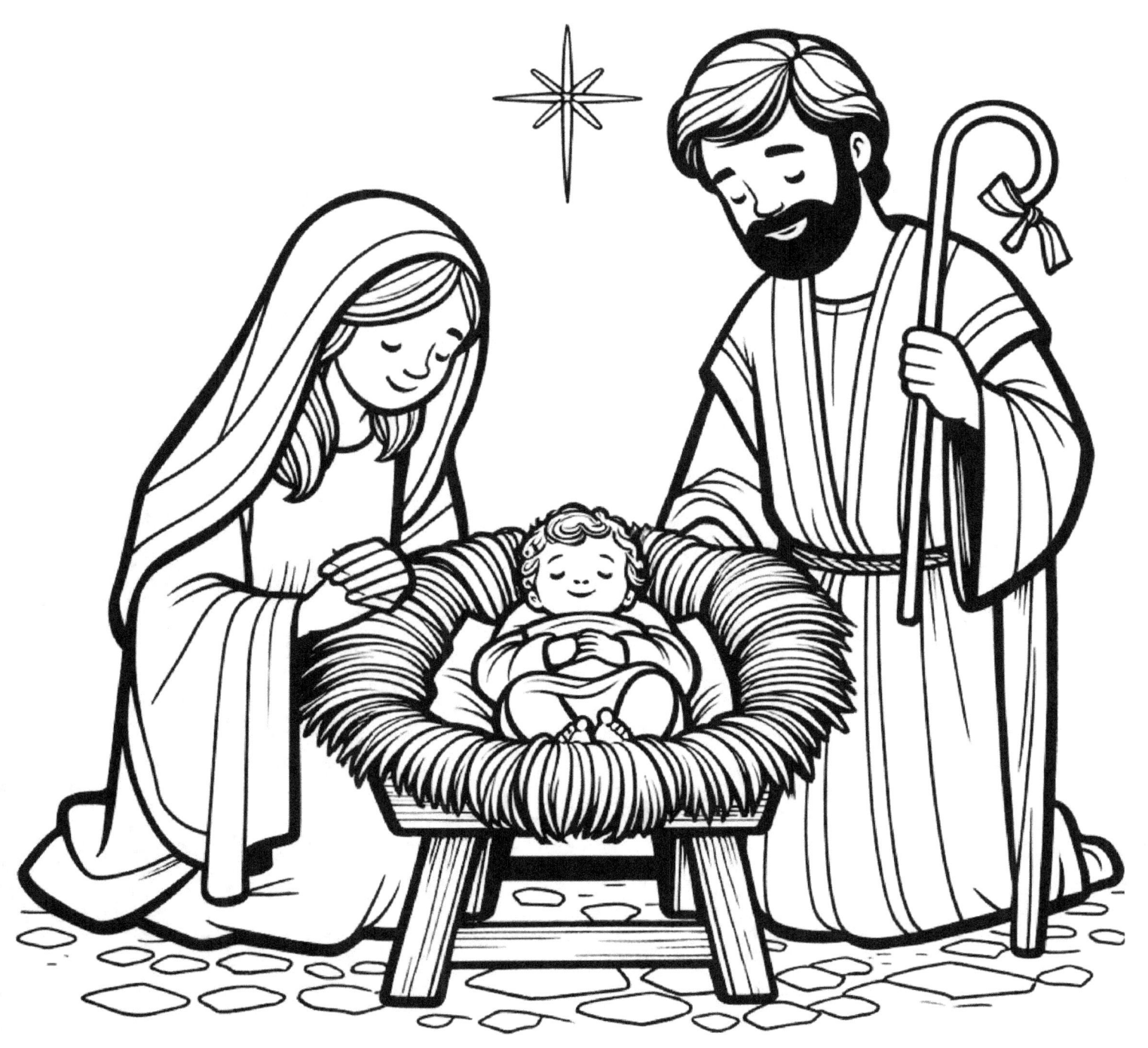

ANGELS REJOICE

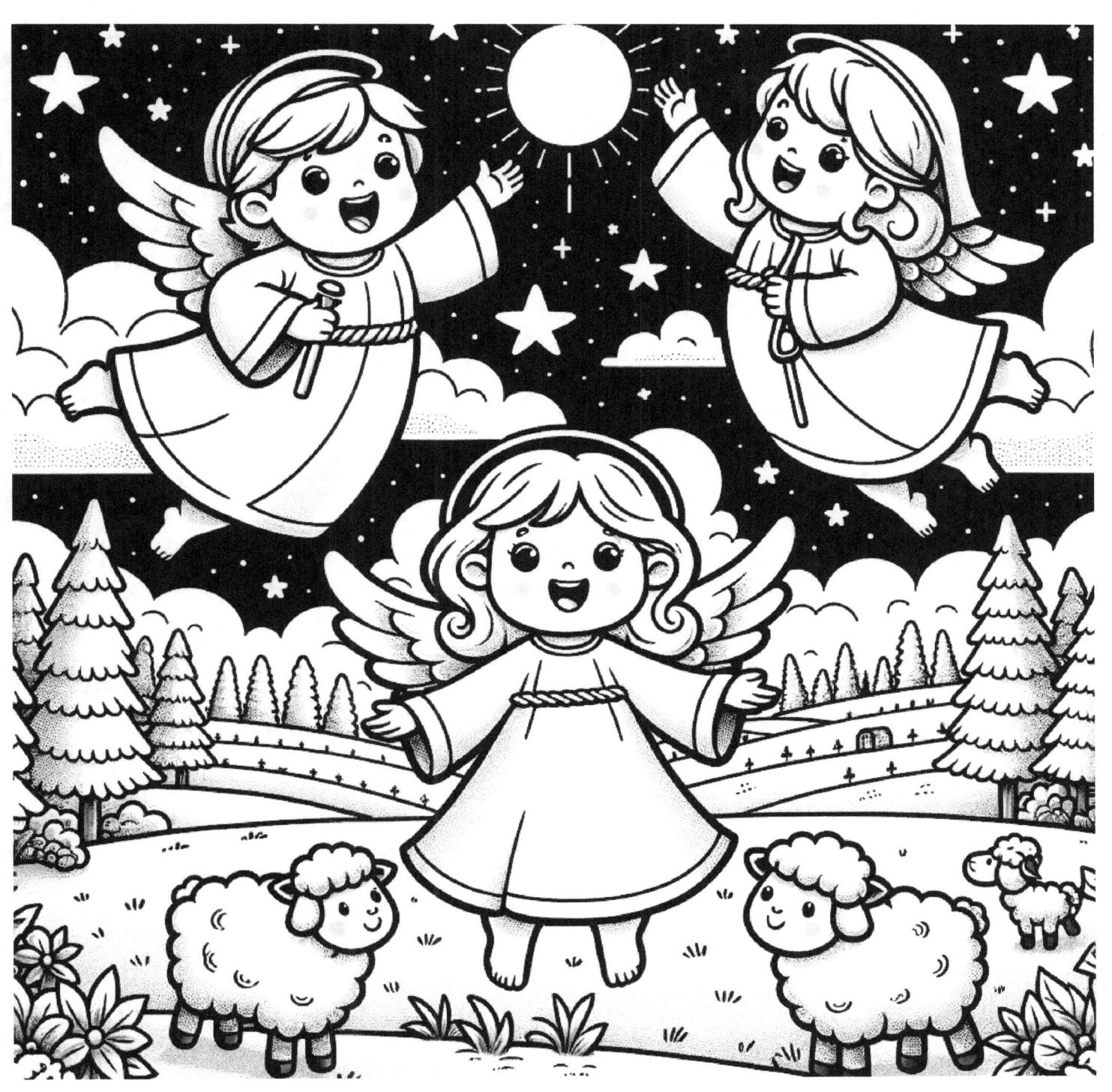

SHEPHERDS ARRIVE

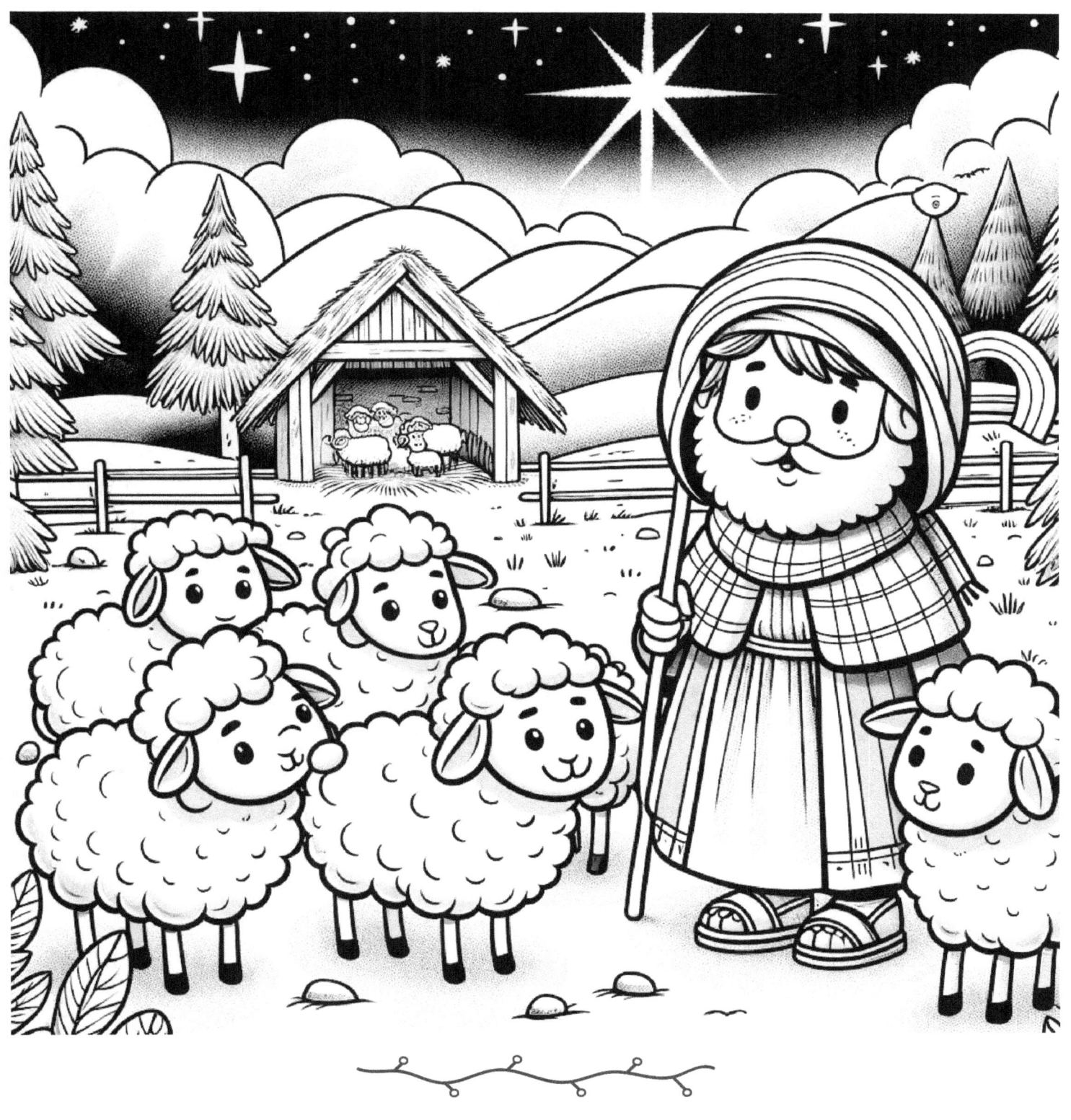

WISE MEN

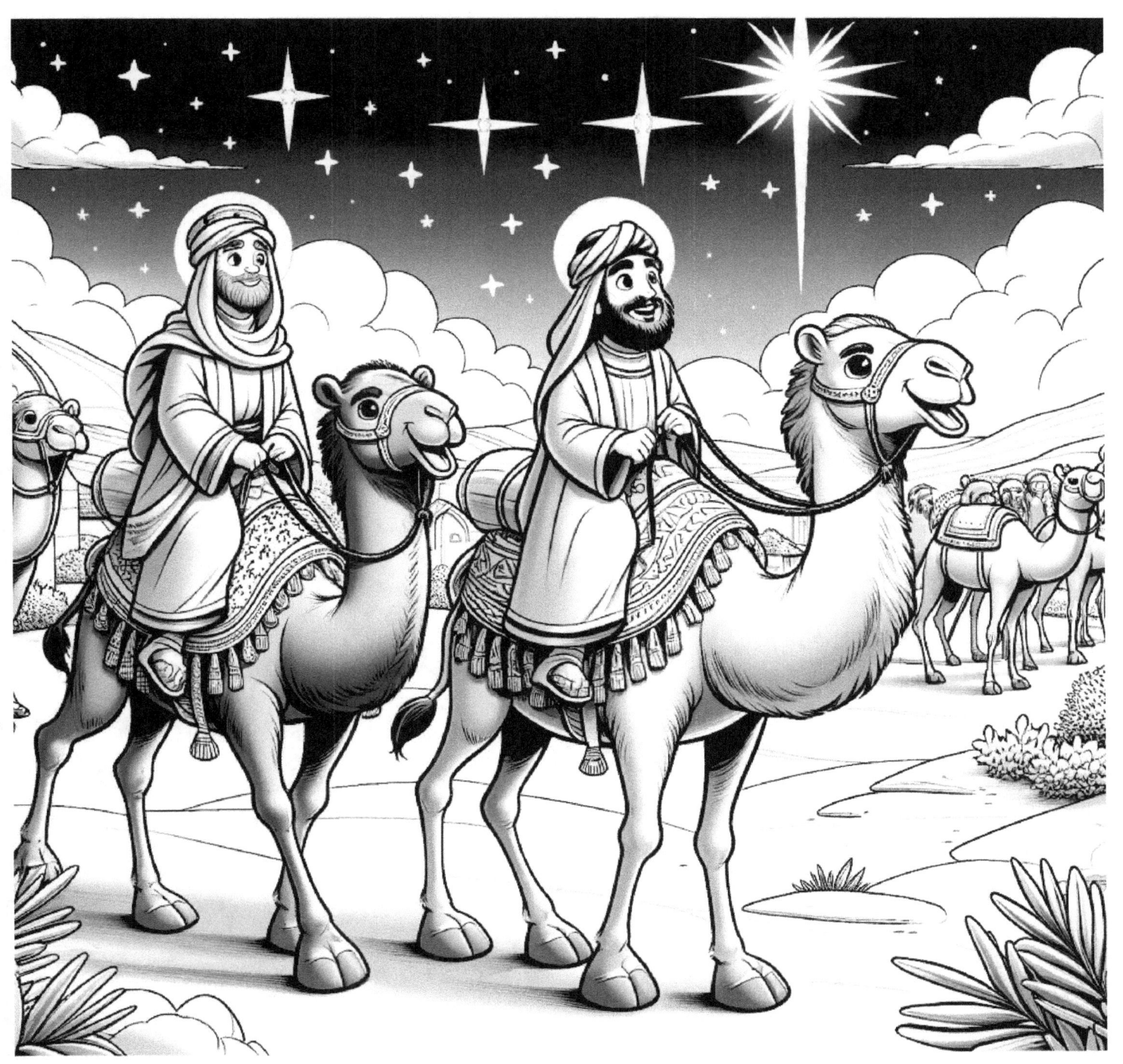

STAR OF BETHLEHAM

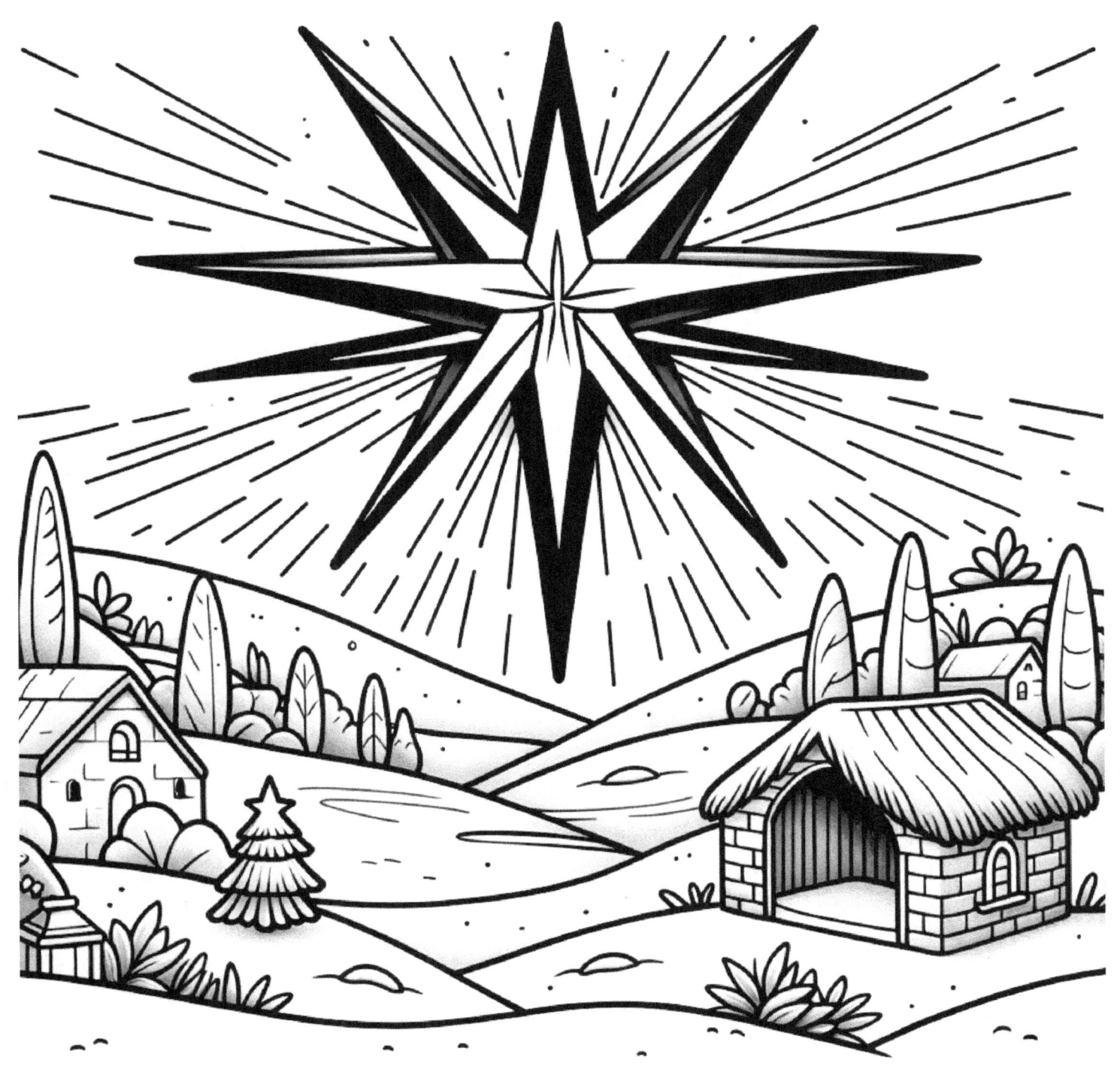

MARY & BABY JESUS

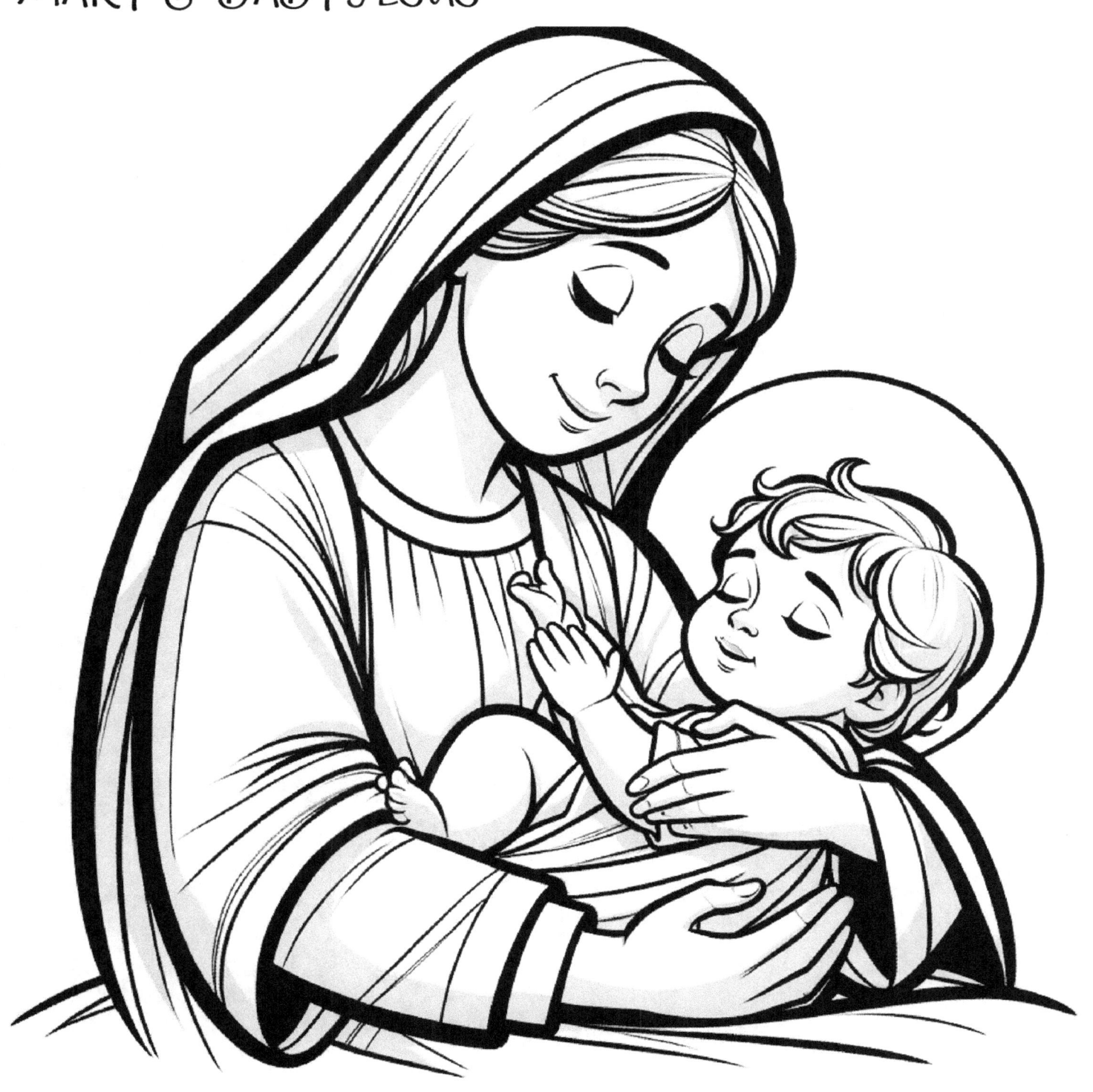

JOSEPH & A DONKEY

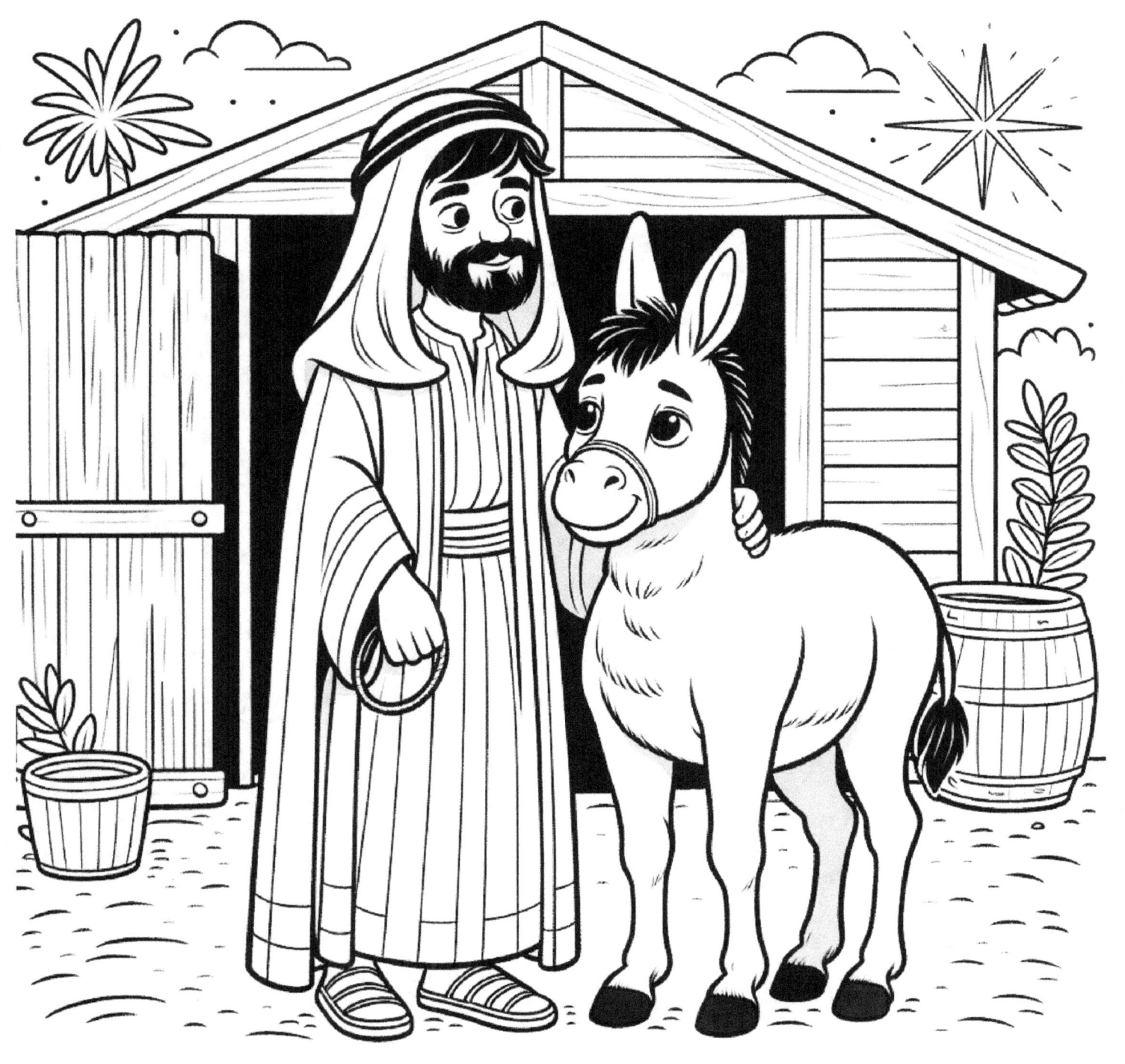

PEACEFUL BETHLEHEM

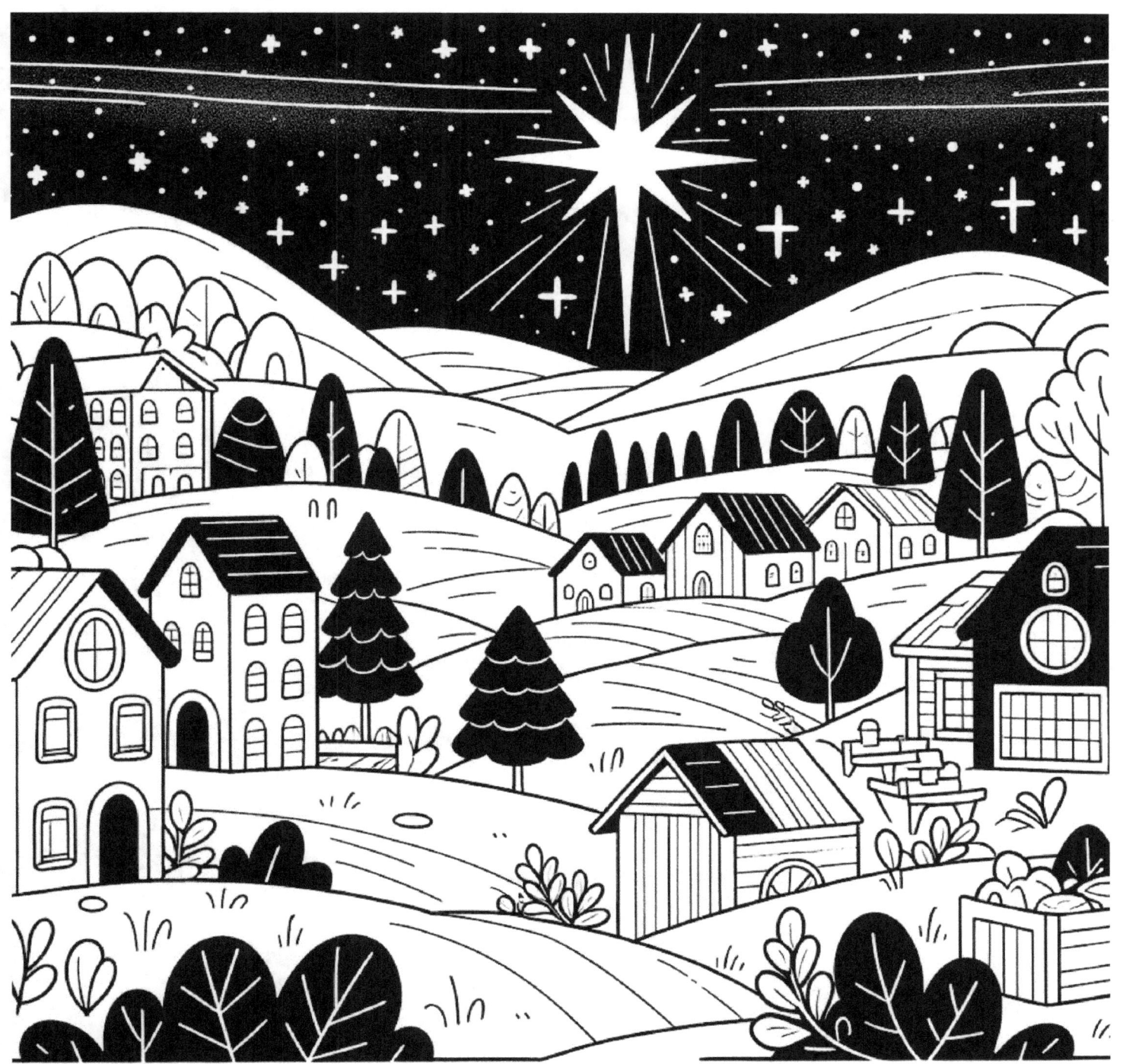

ANGELS

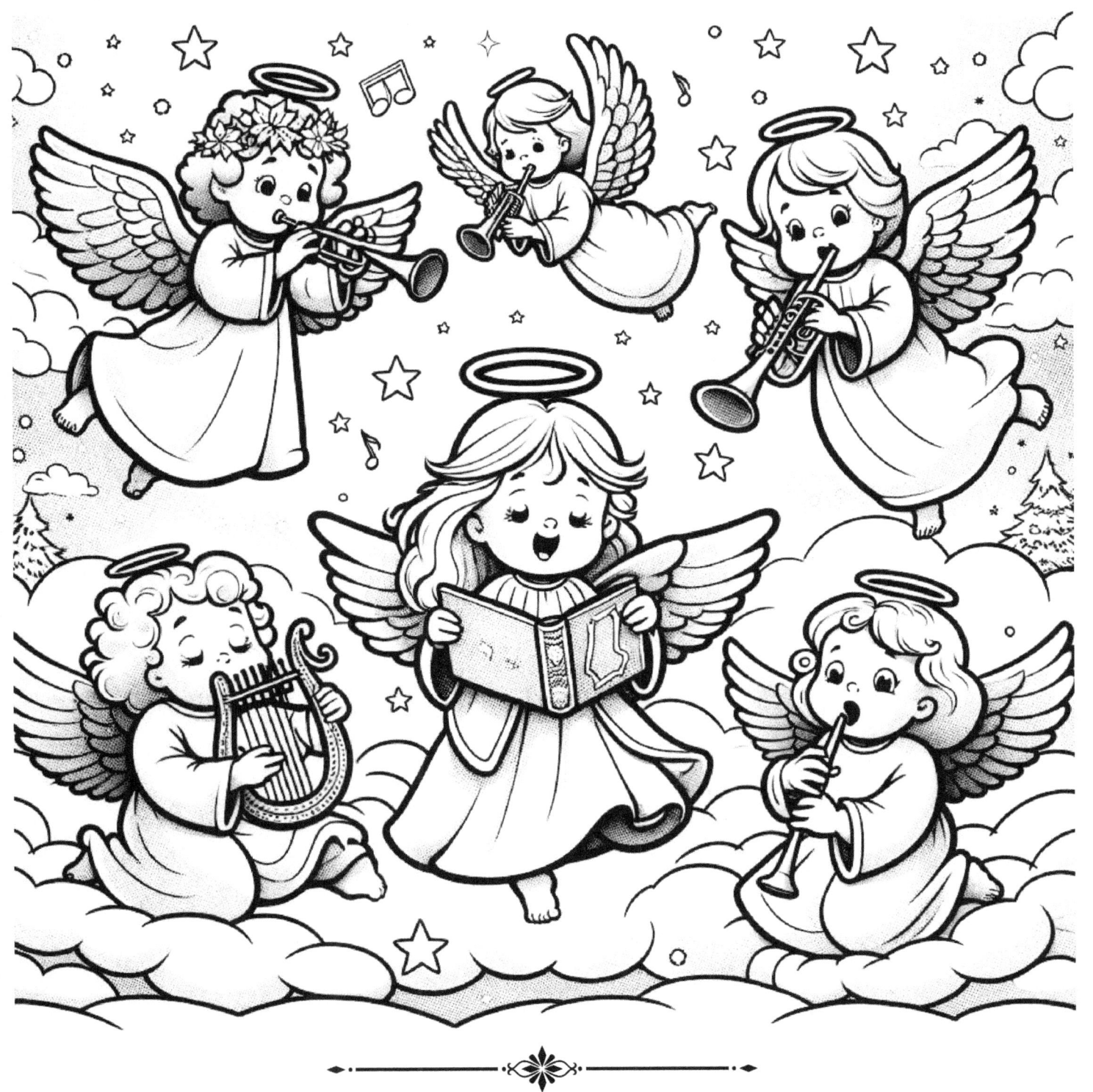

VISITING BABY JESUS

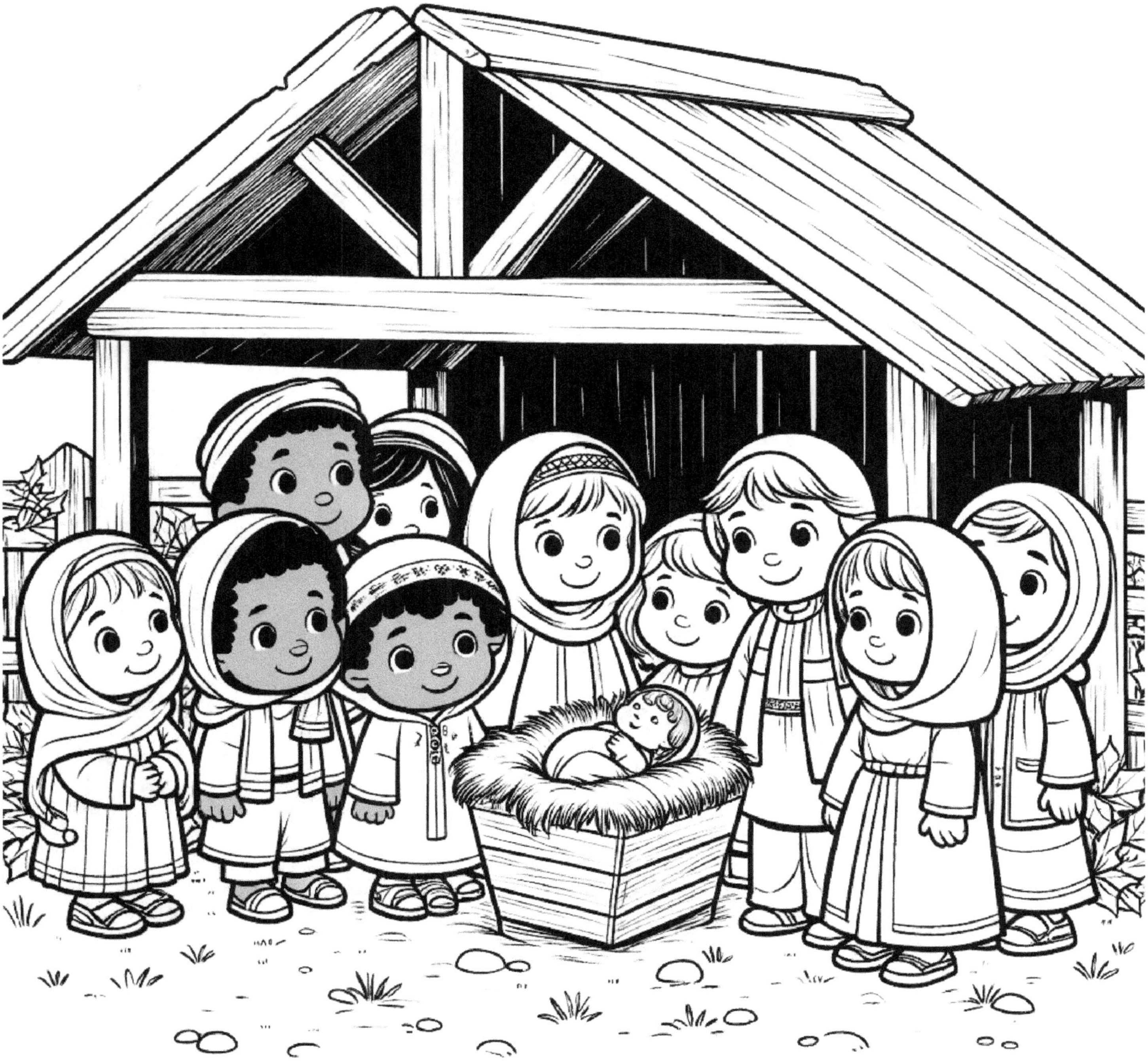

SHEEP GRAZING

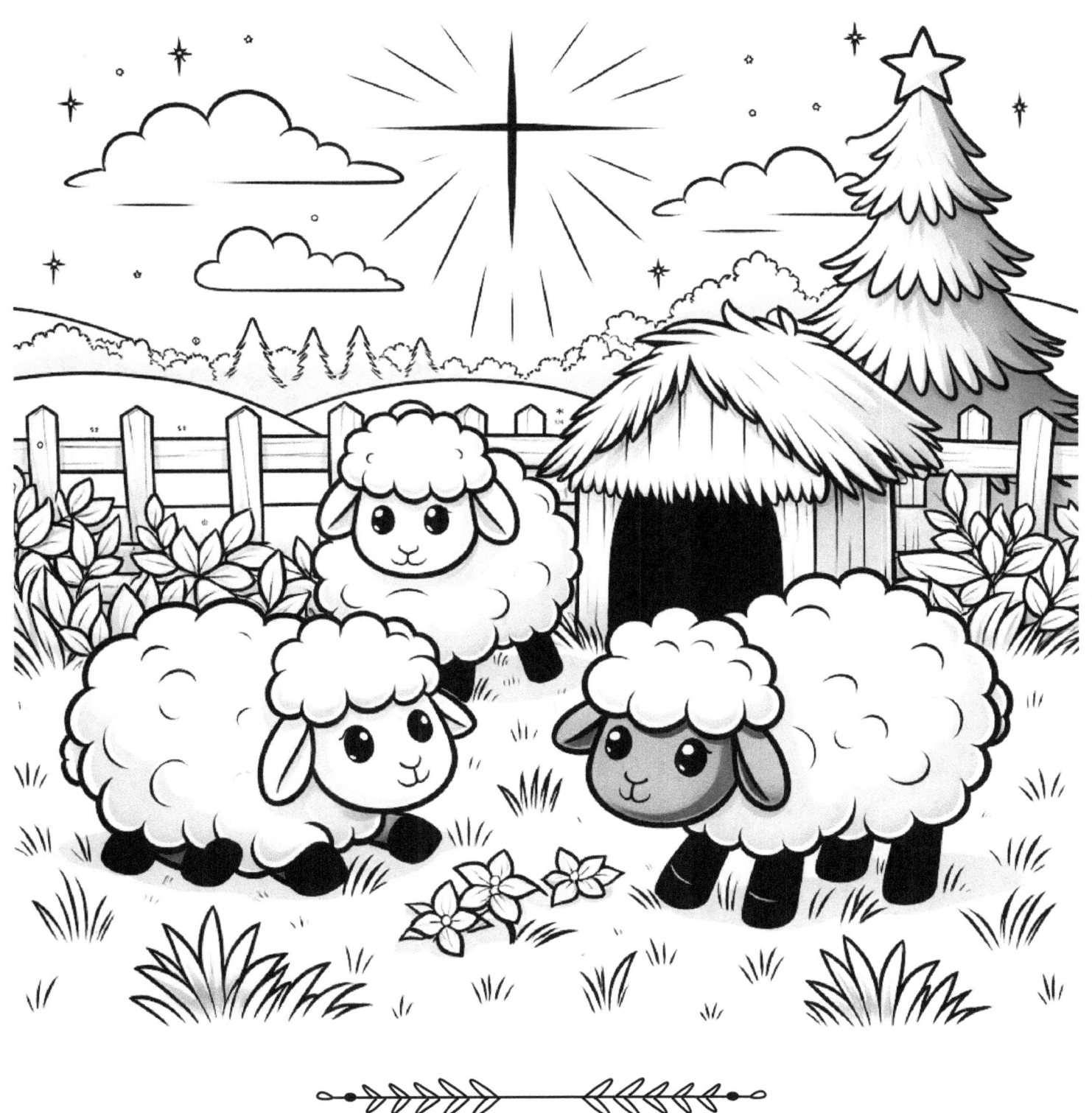

THREE WISE MEN

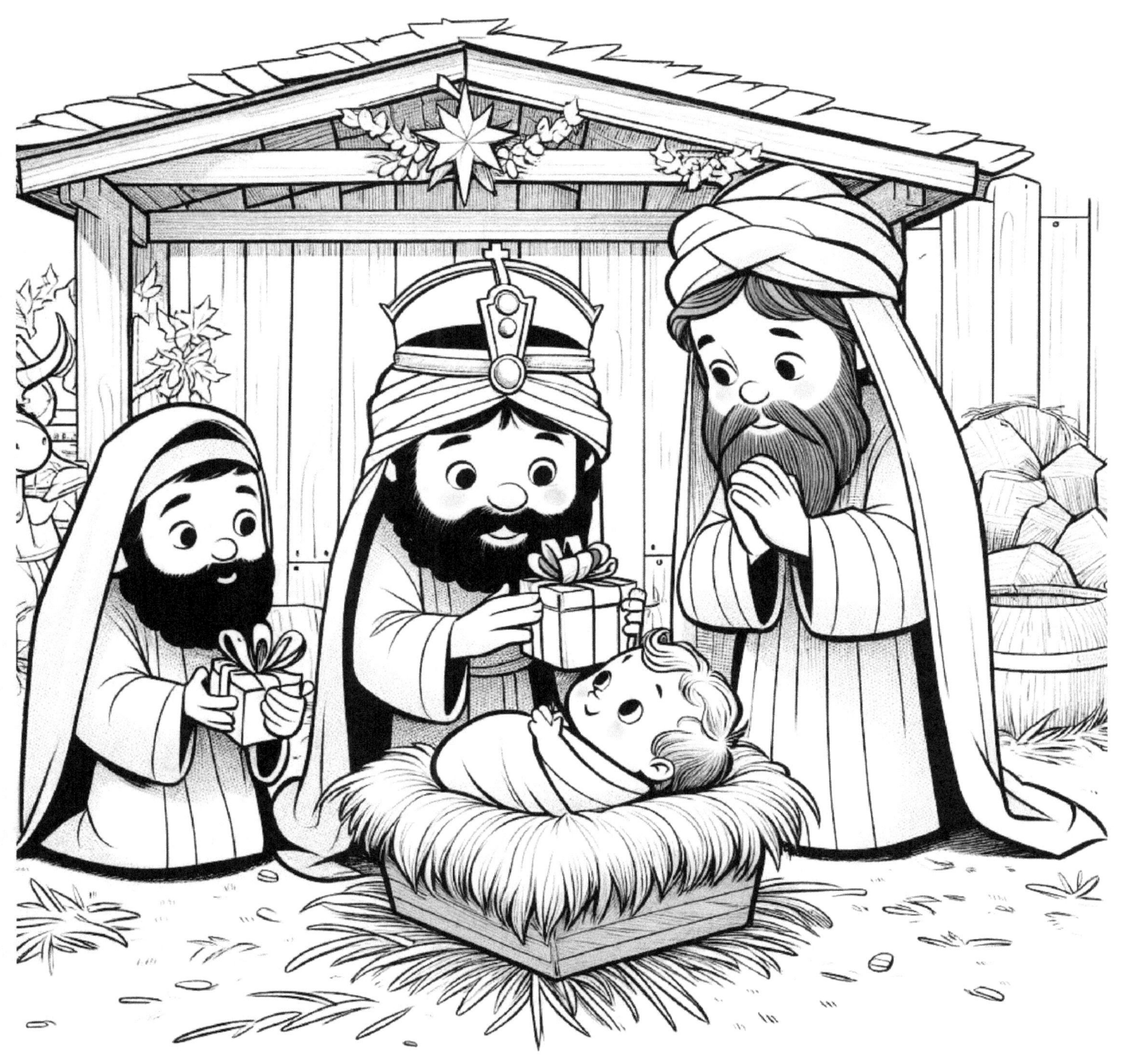

STABLE

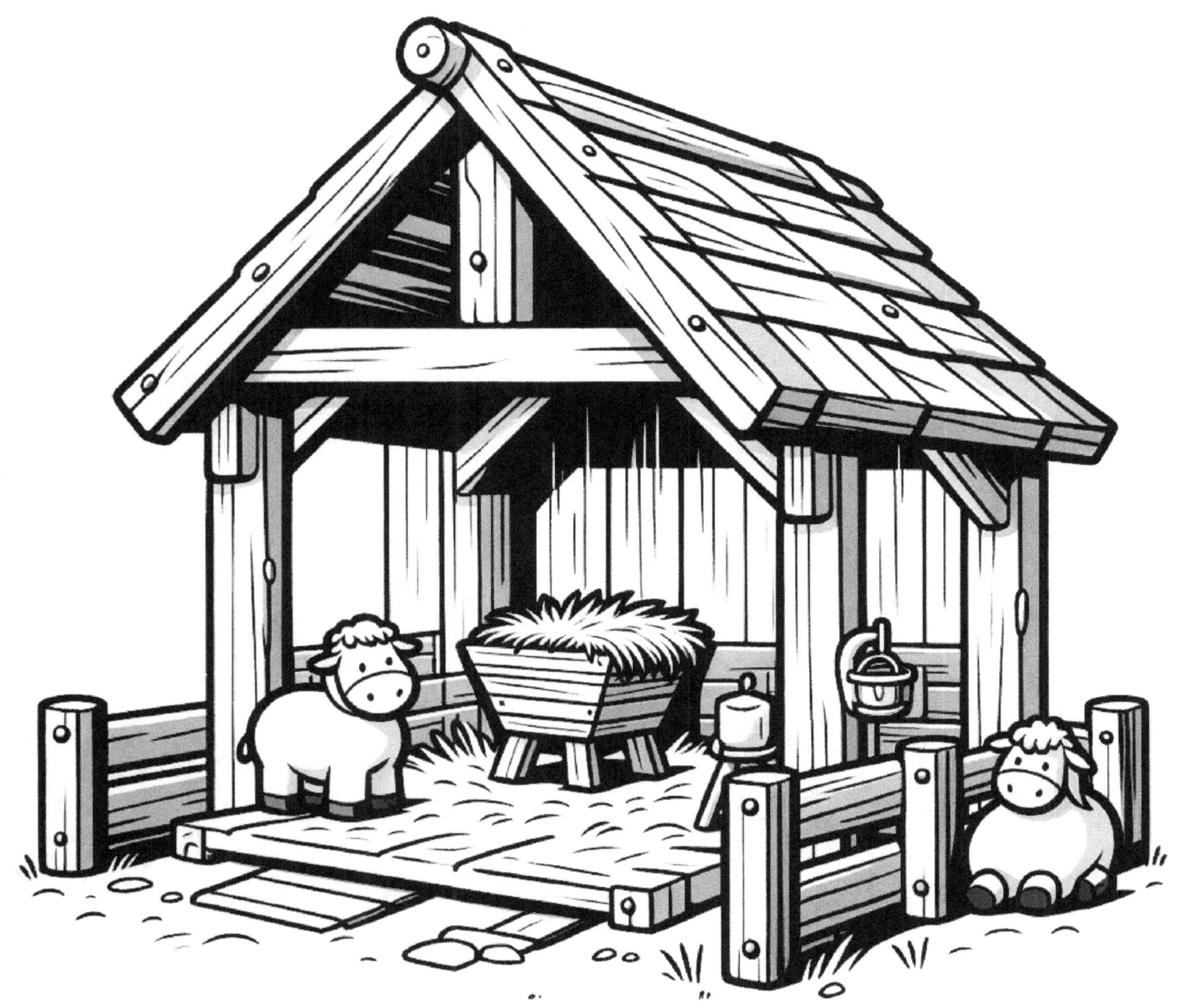

ANGEL

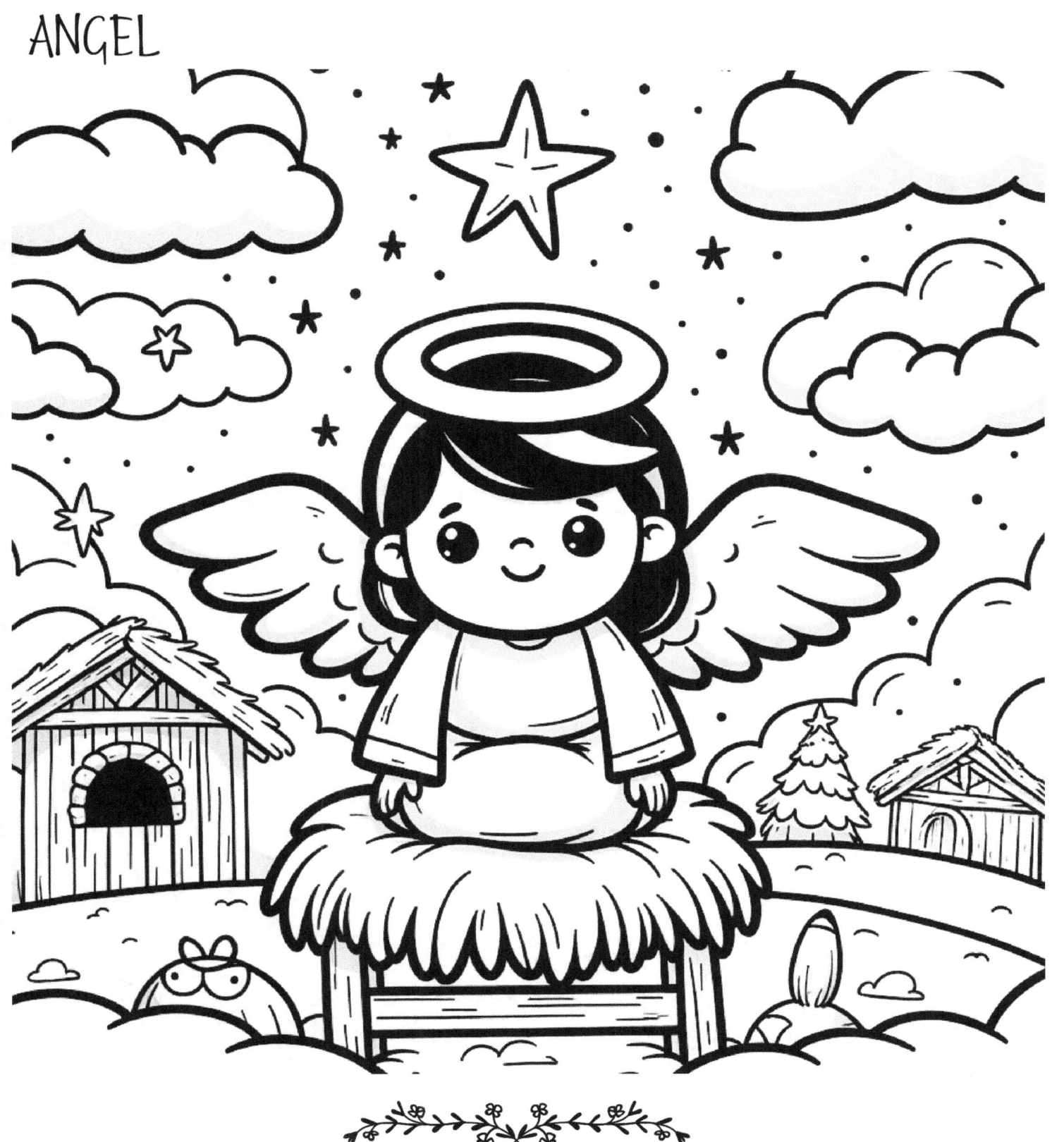

ANIMALS

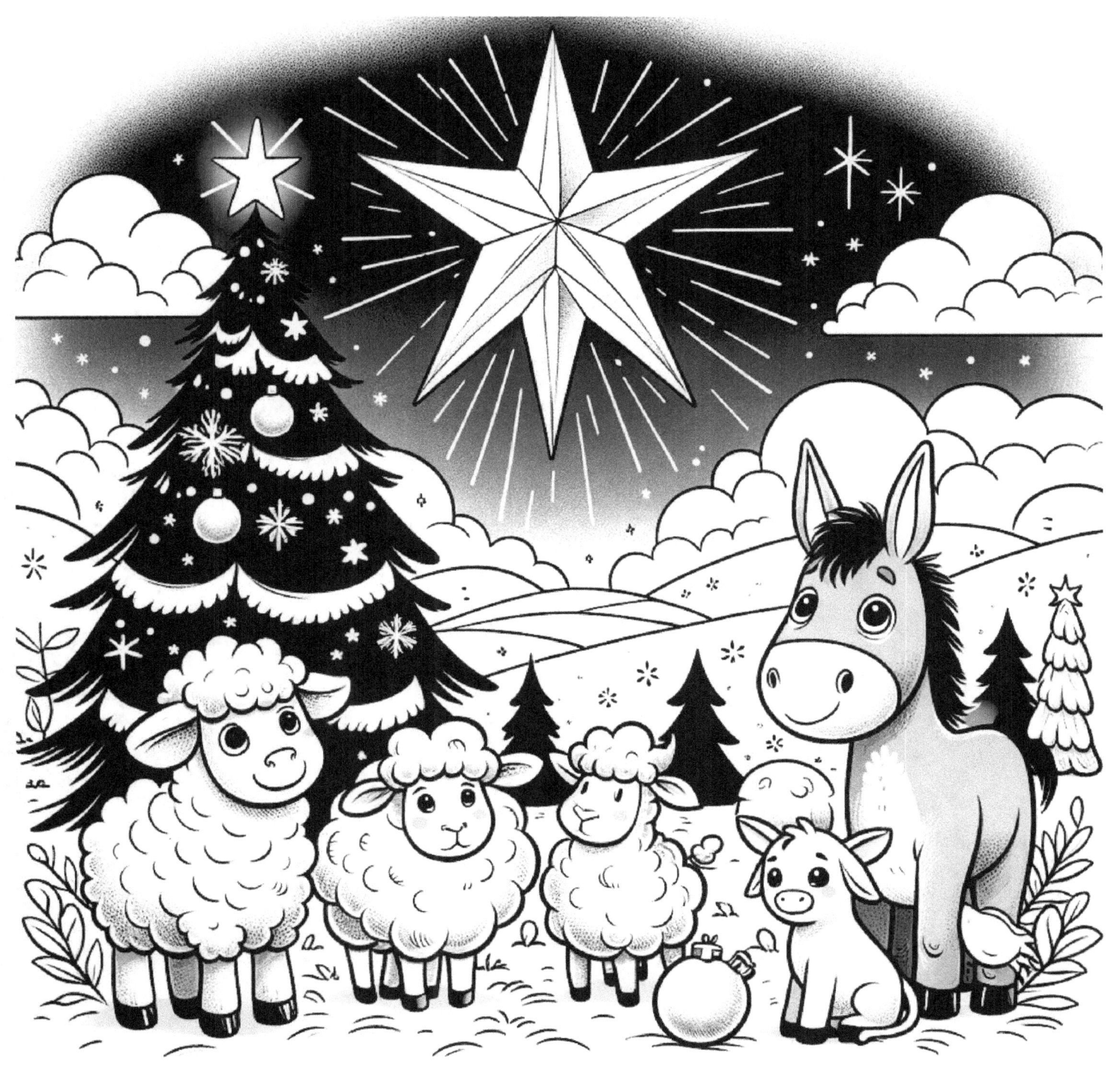

SHEPHERDS

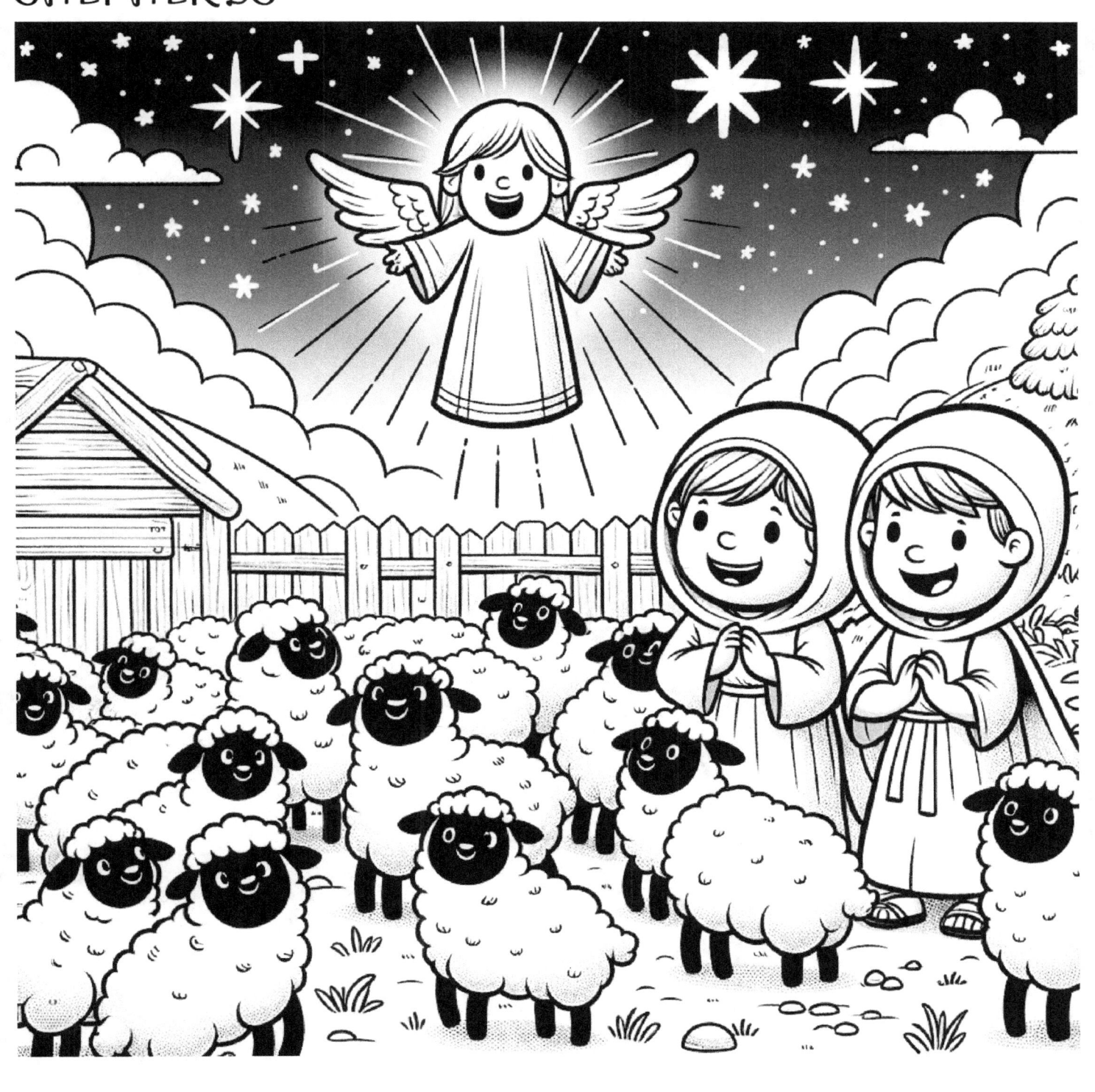

NATIVITY

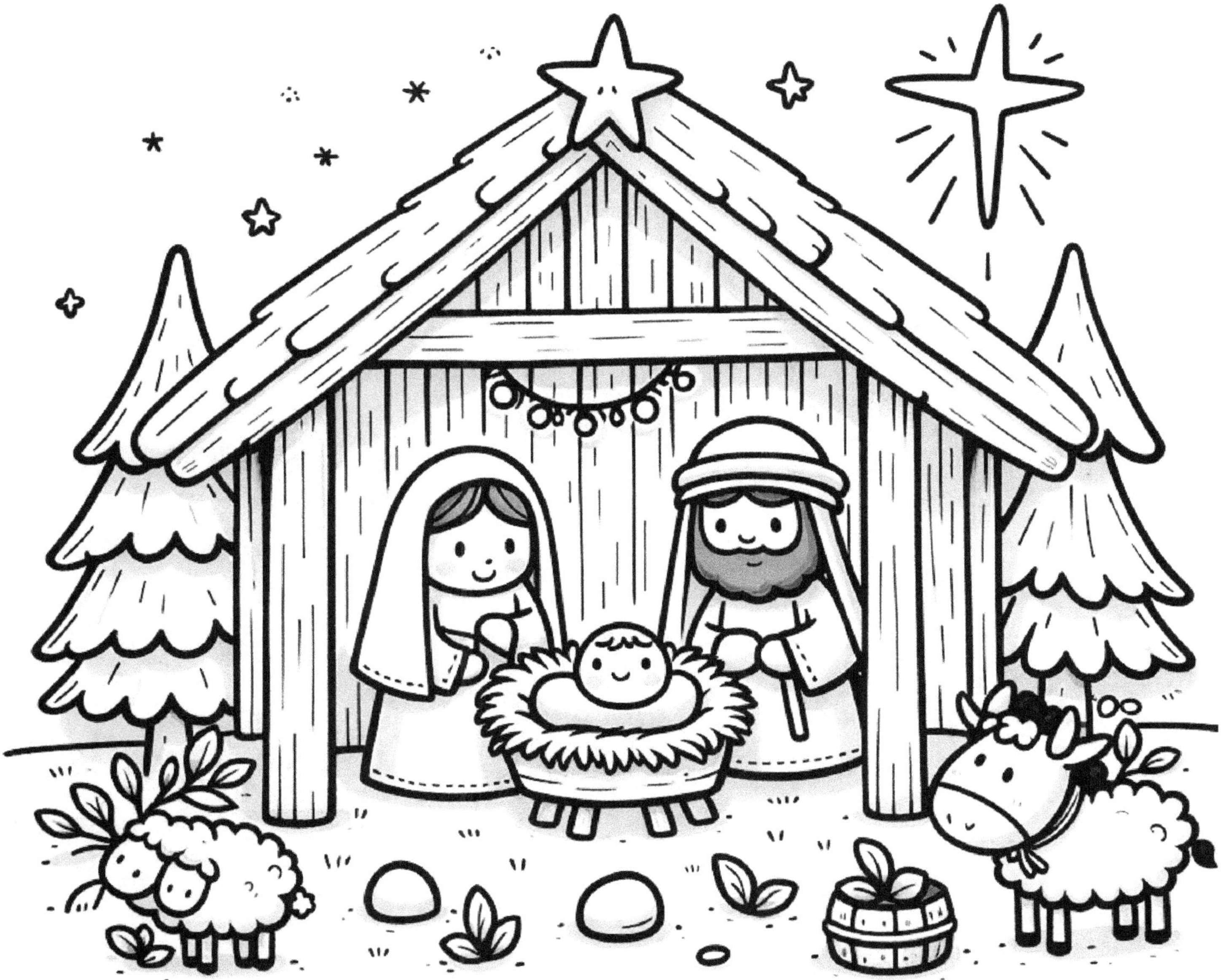

STAR OF BETHLEHAM

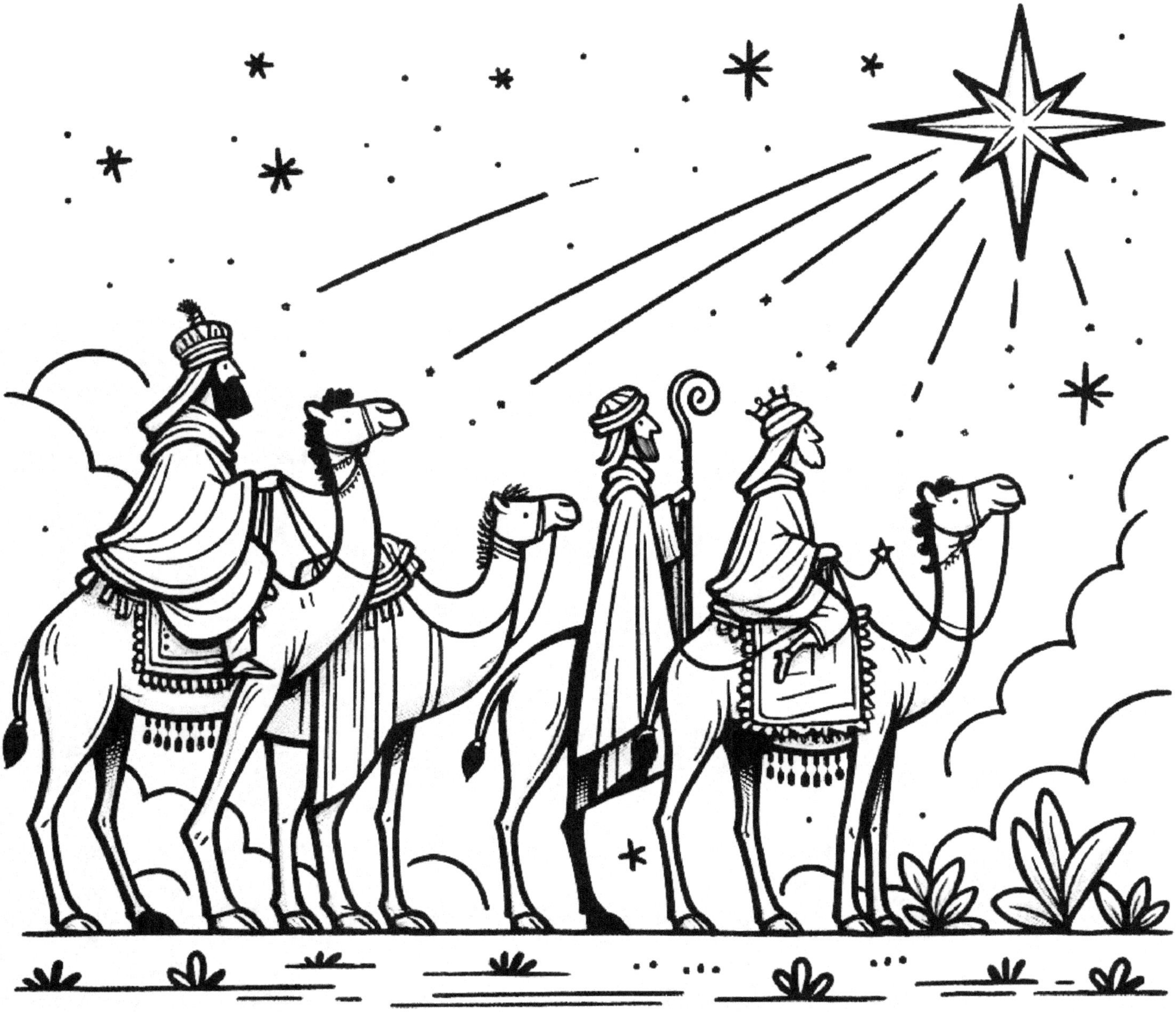

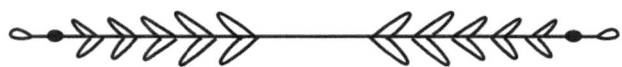

ANGELS & SHEEP

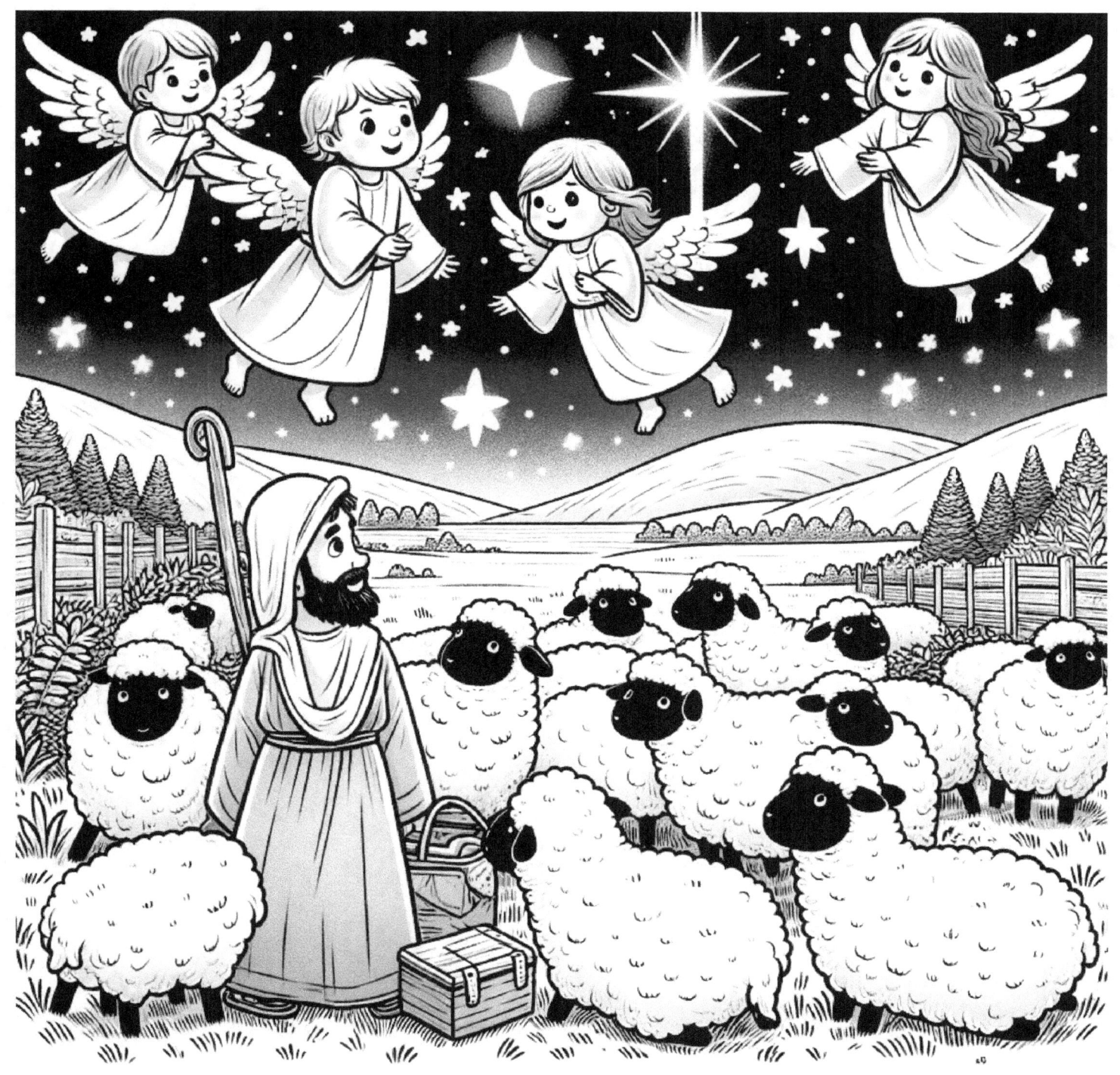

MARY & JOSEPH

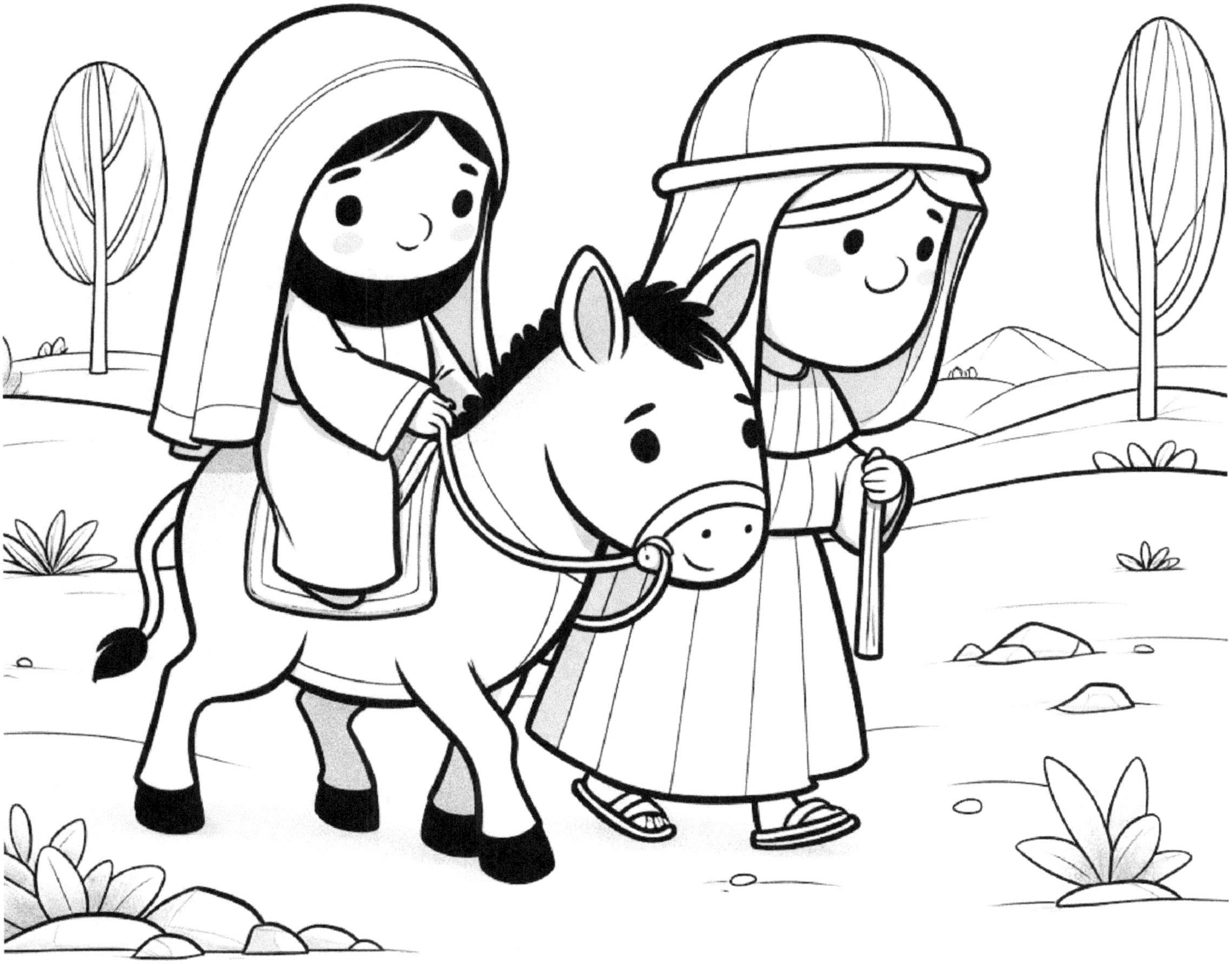

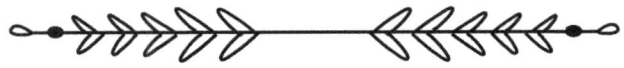

ANGEL & MARY

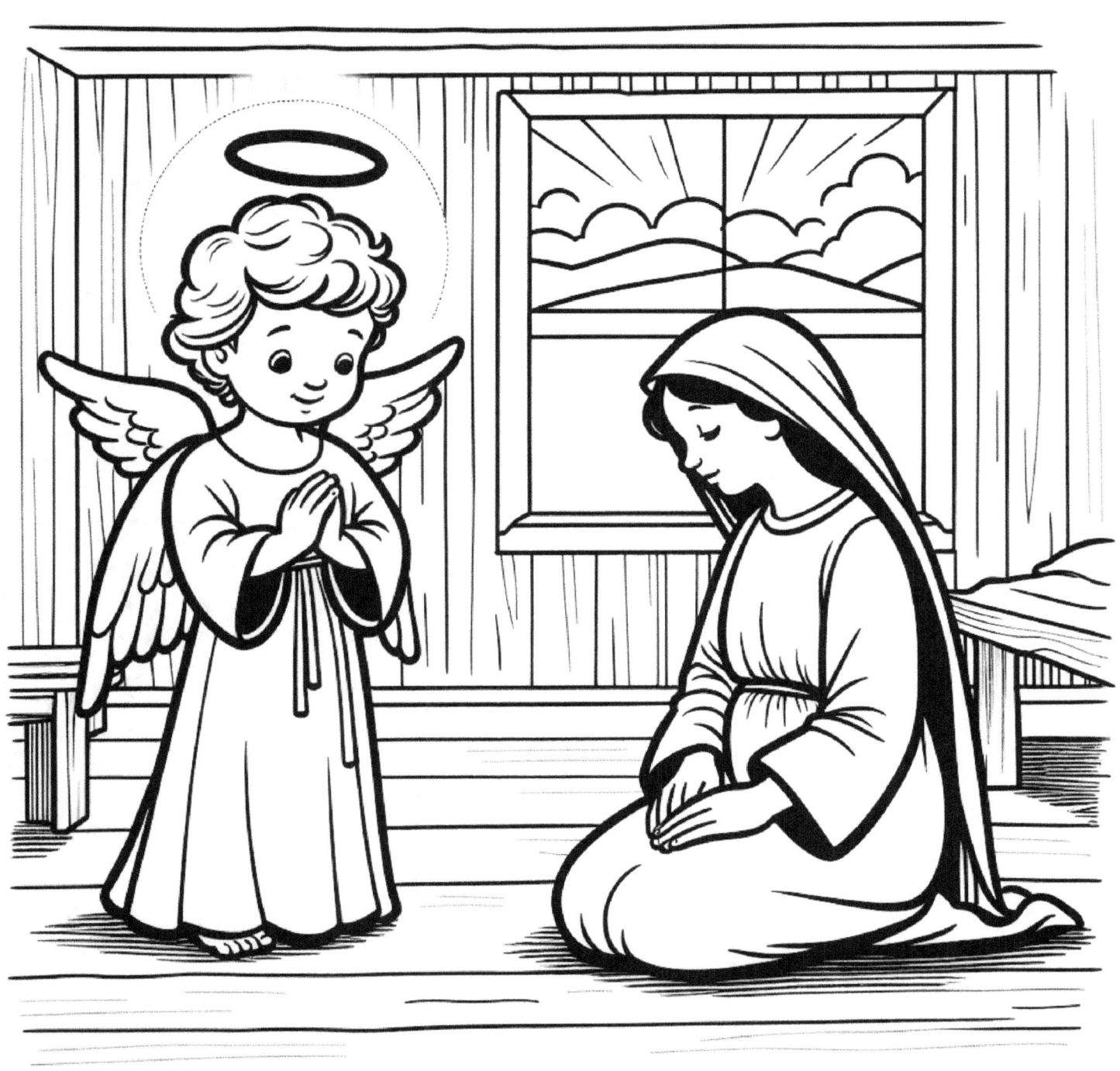

MARY & ELIZABETH

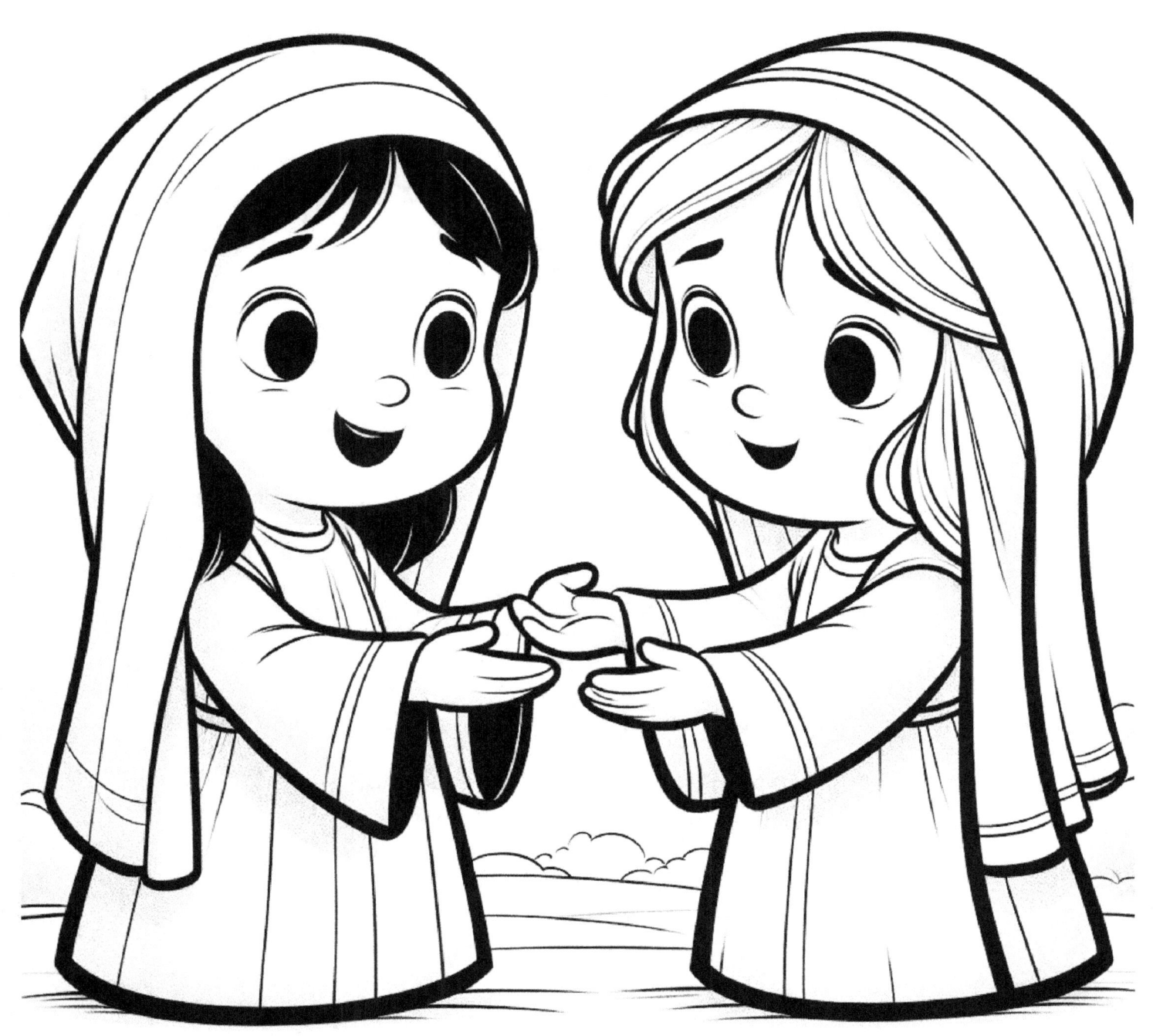

SIMEON & ANNA

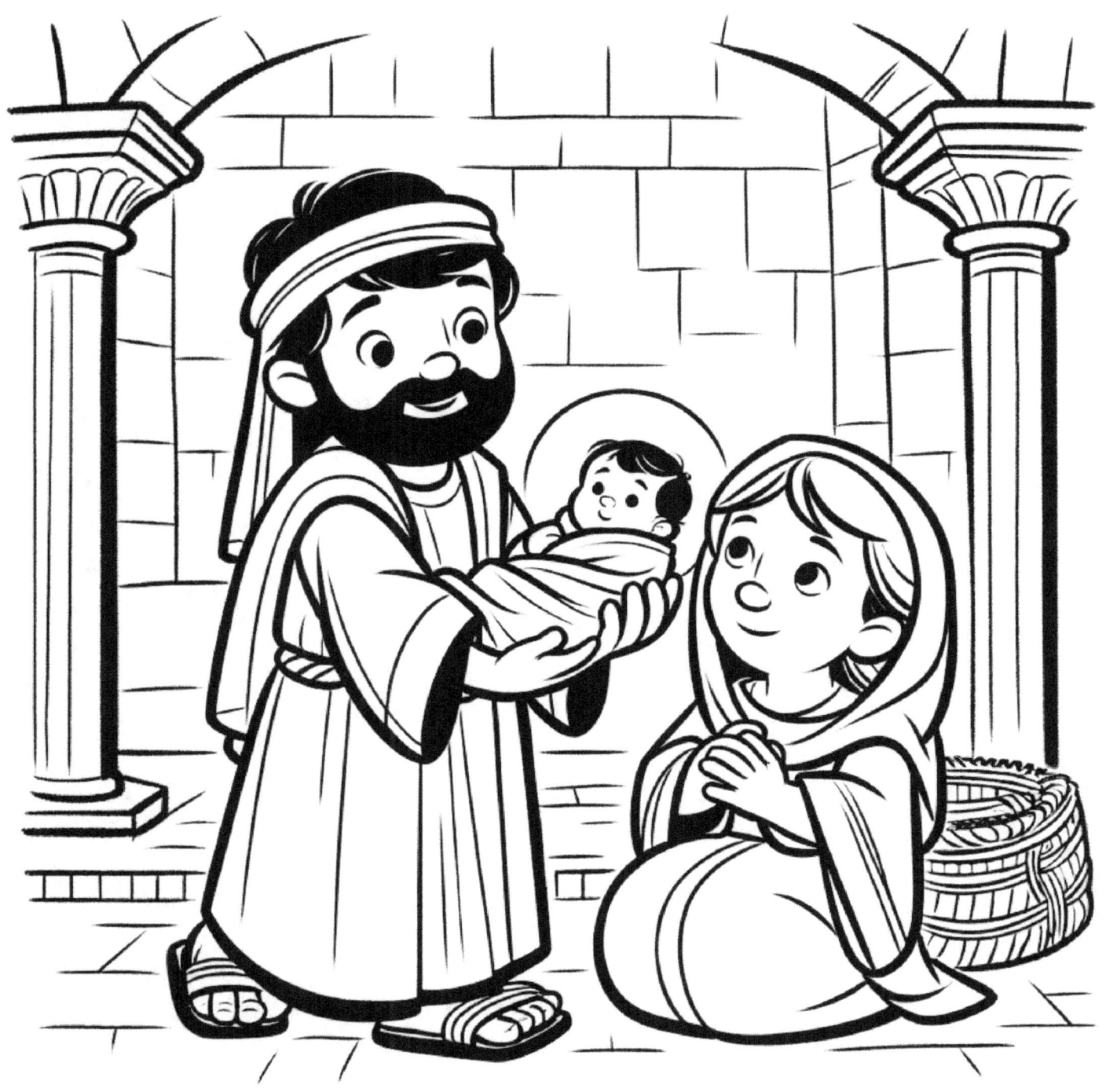

FLIGHT TO EGYPT

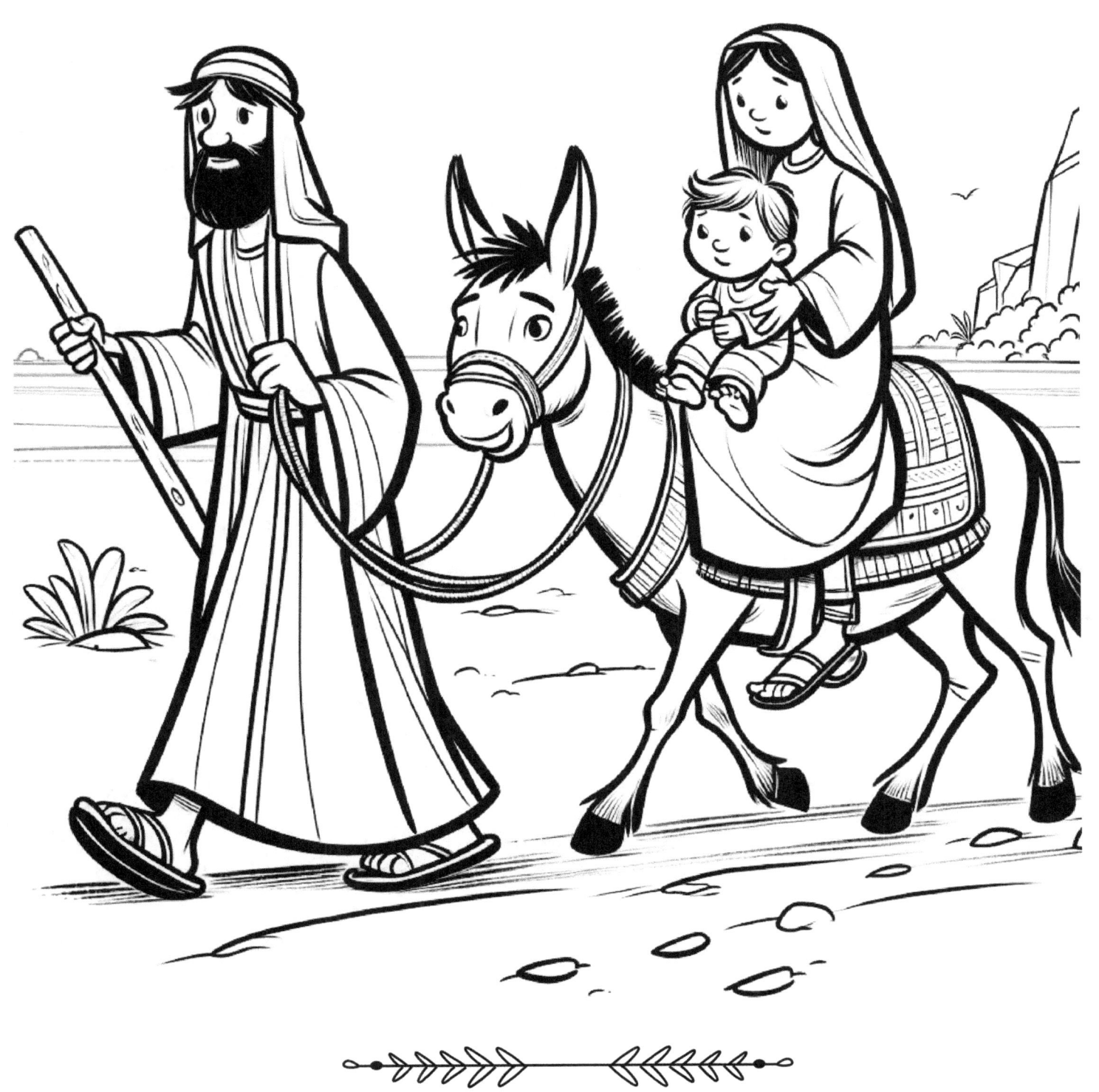

SHEPHERDS

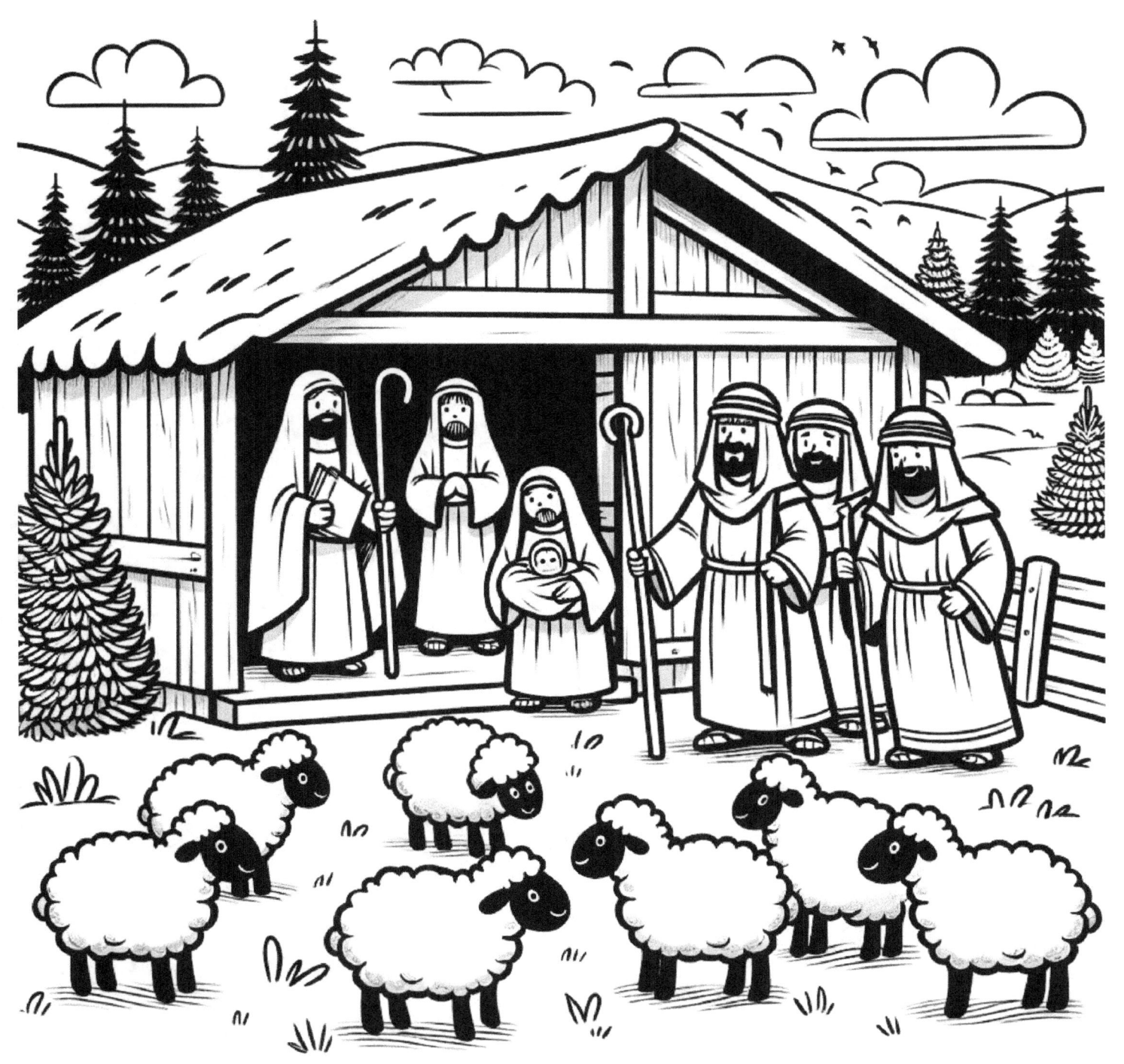

NATIVITY ANIMALS

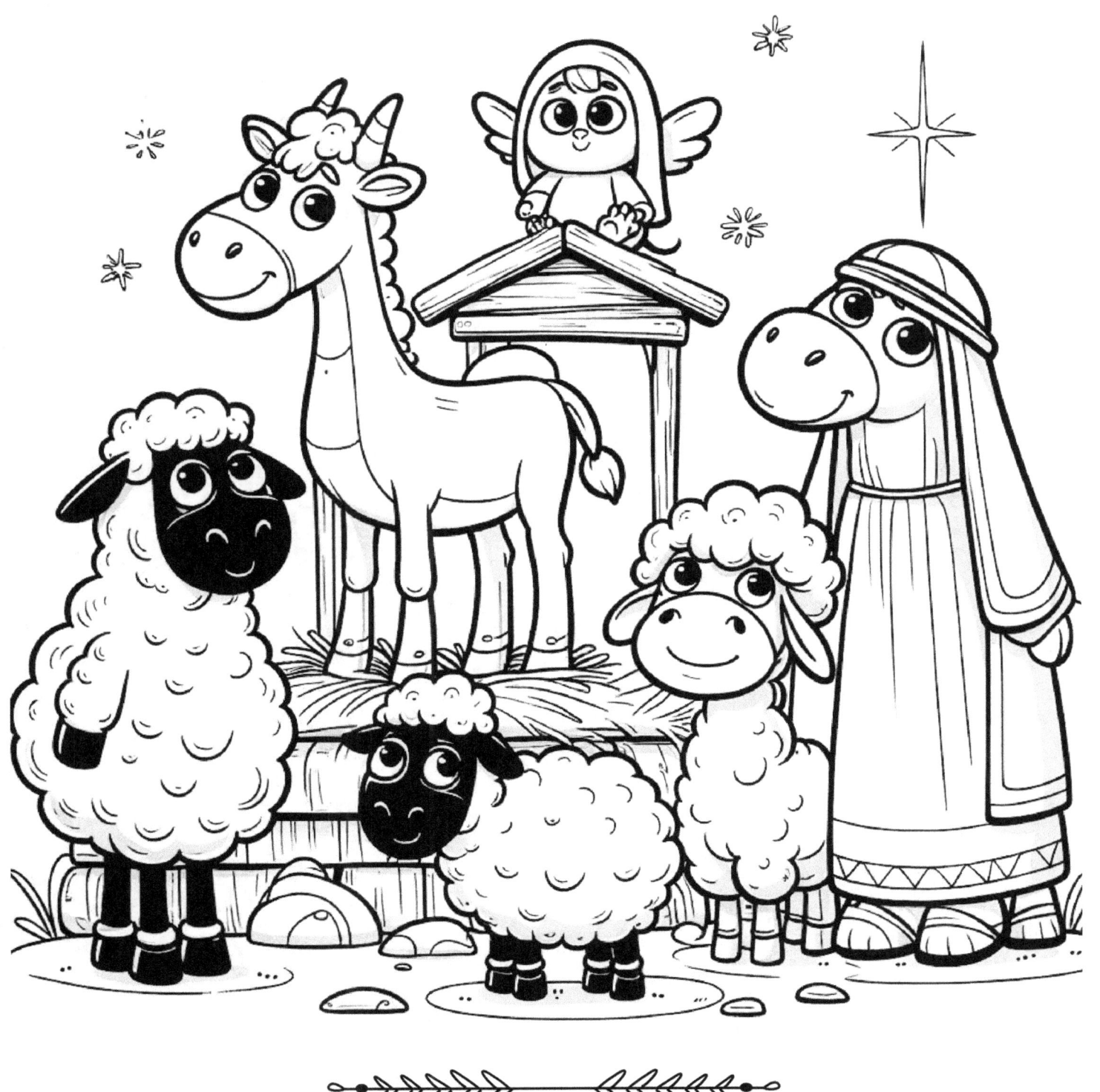

VILLAGE

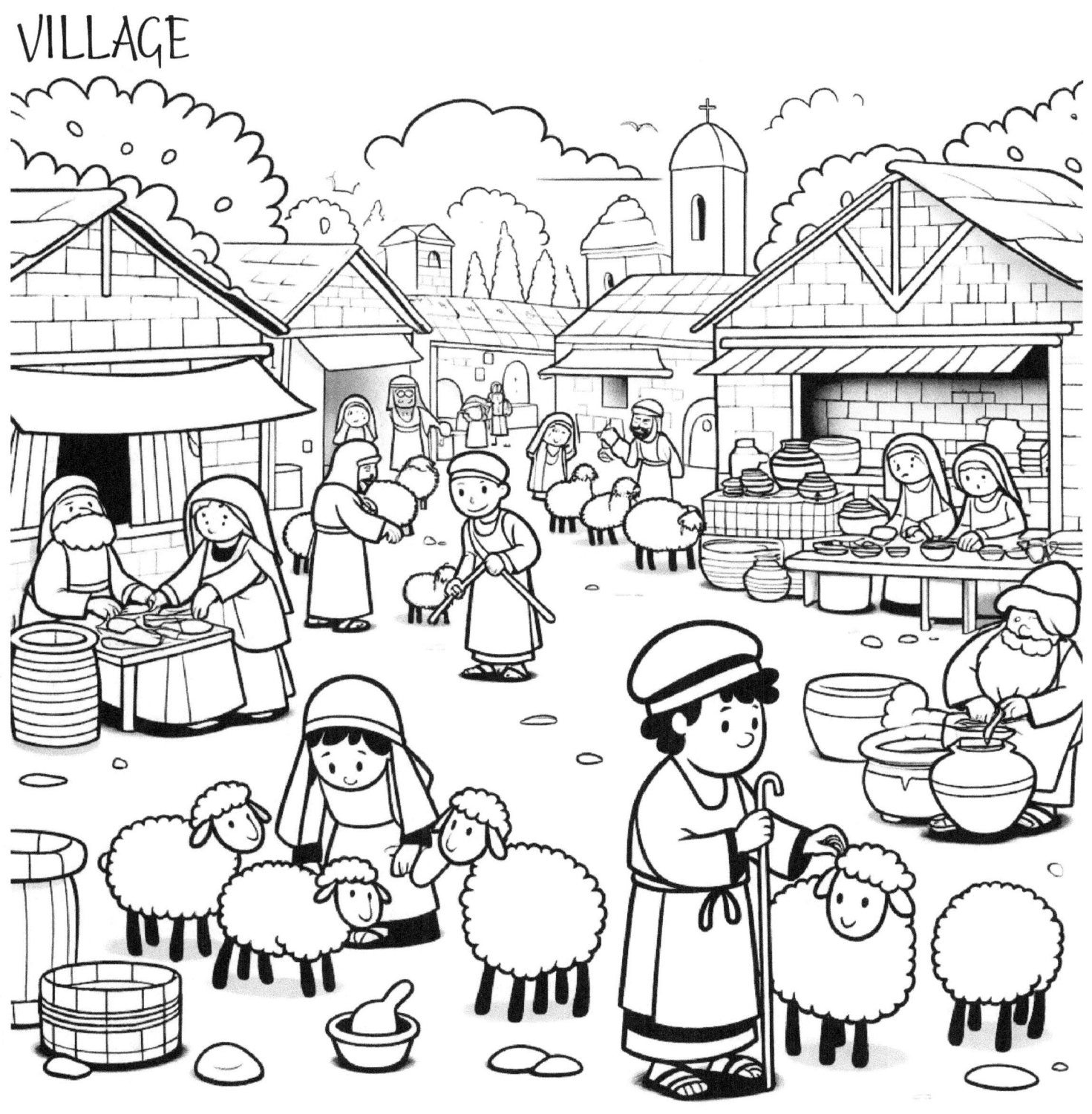

BETHLEHEM TREE

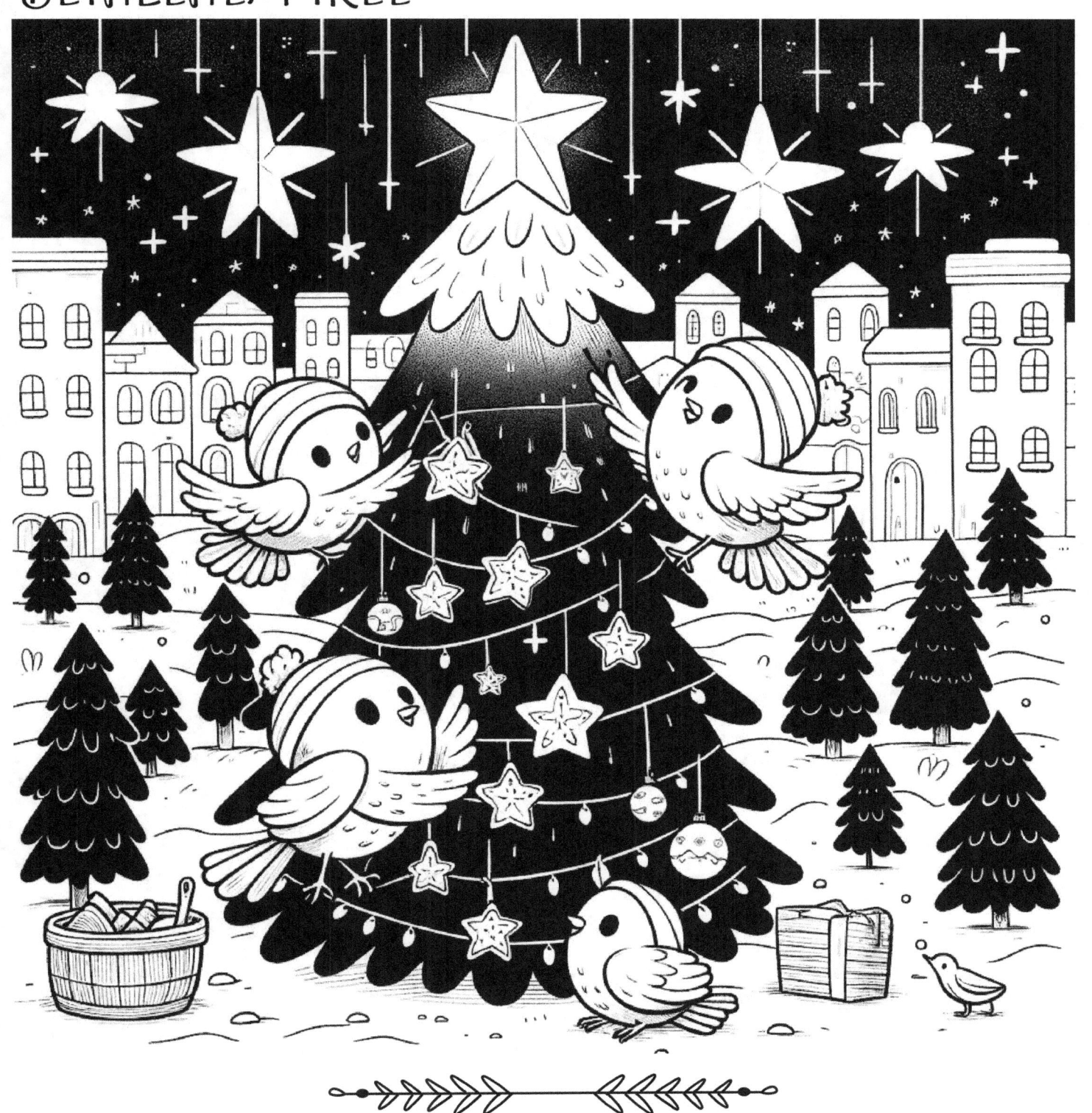

MUSICAL INSTRUMENTS

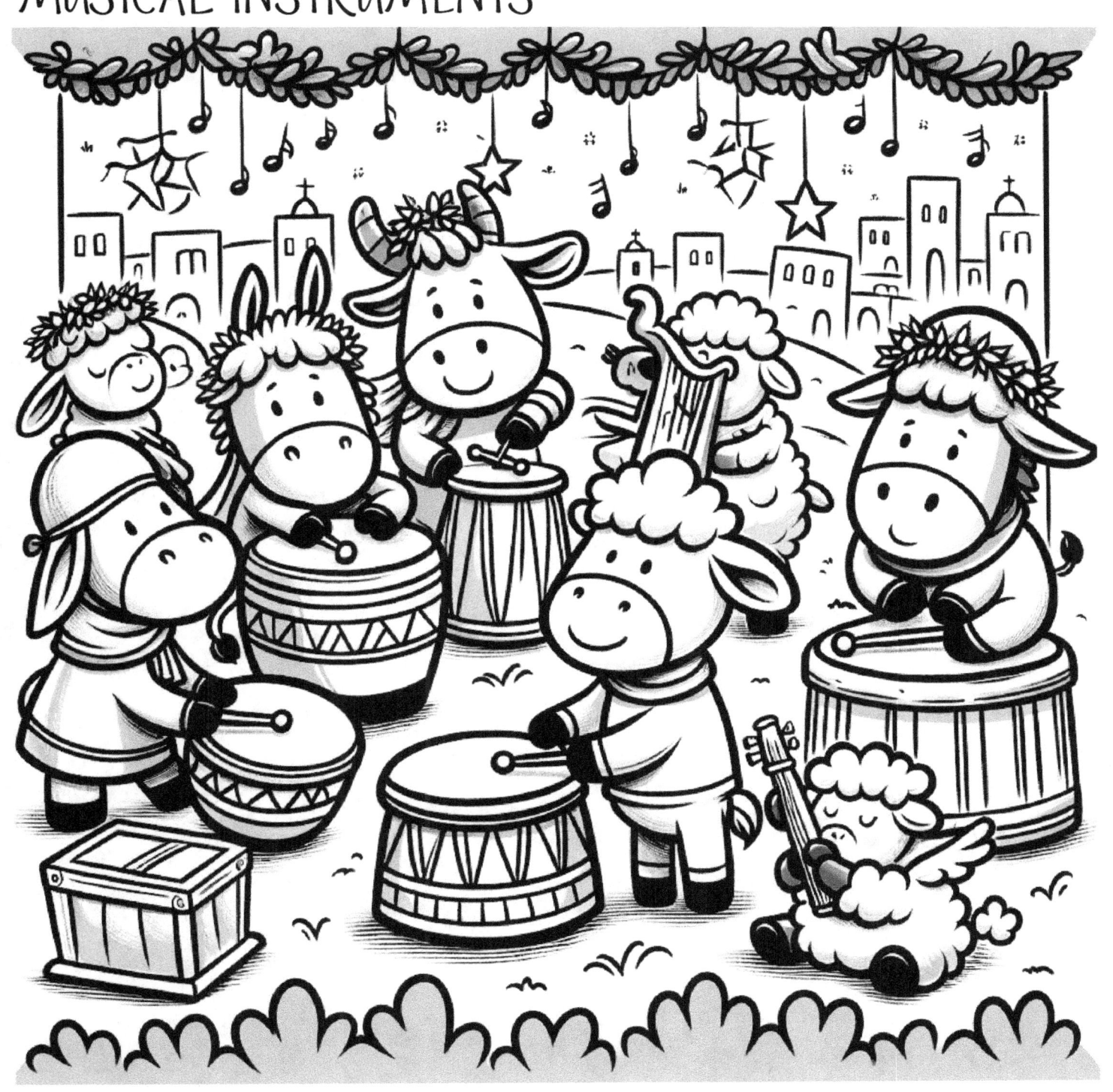

MARKET

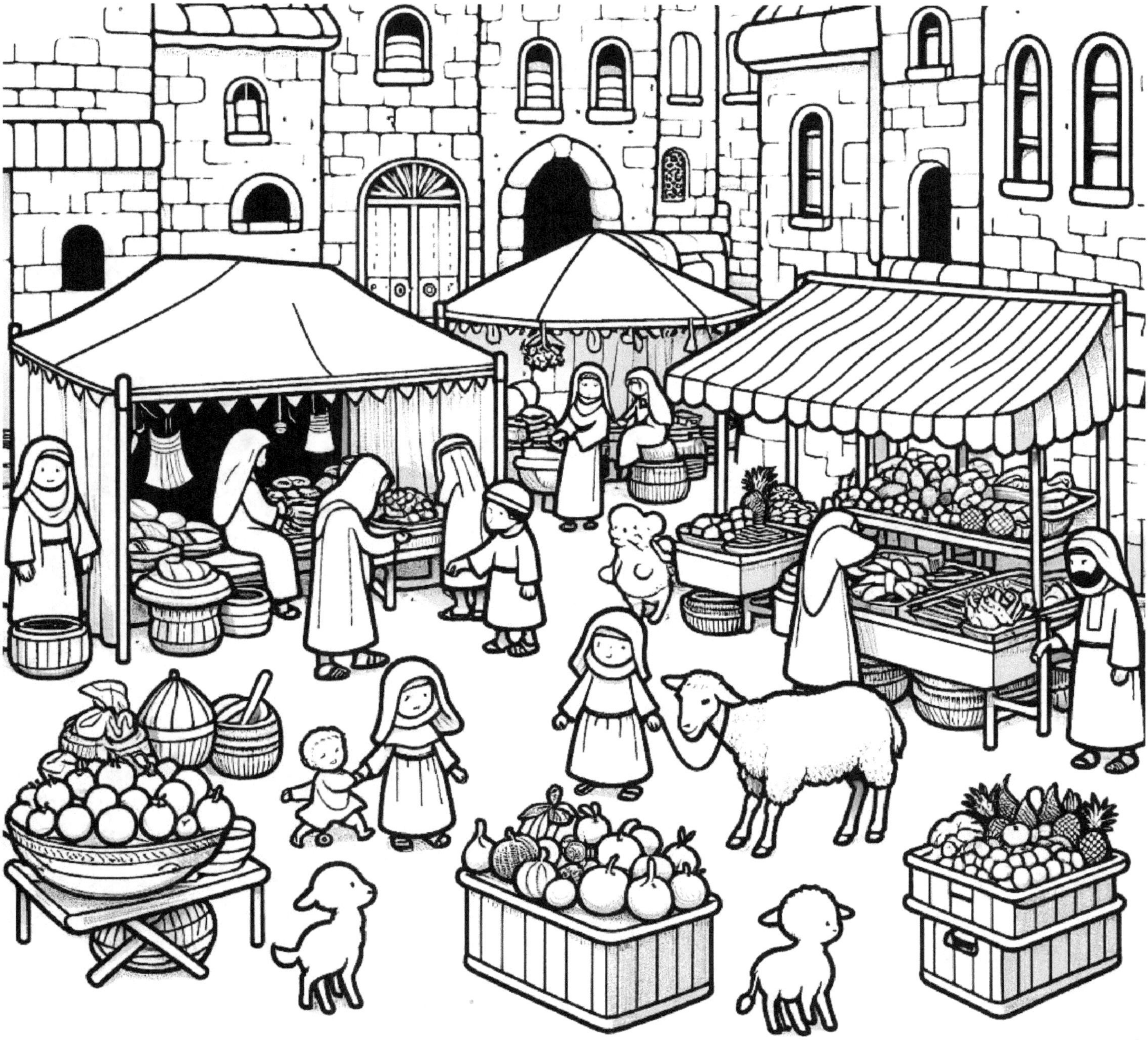

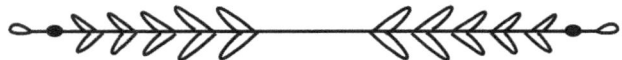

ANGELS REJOICING

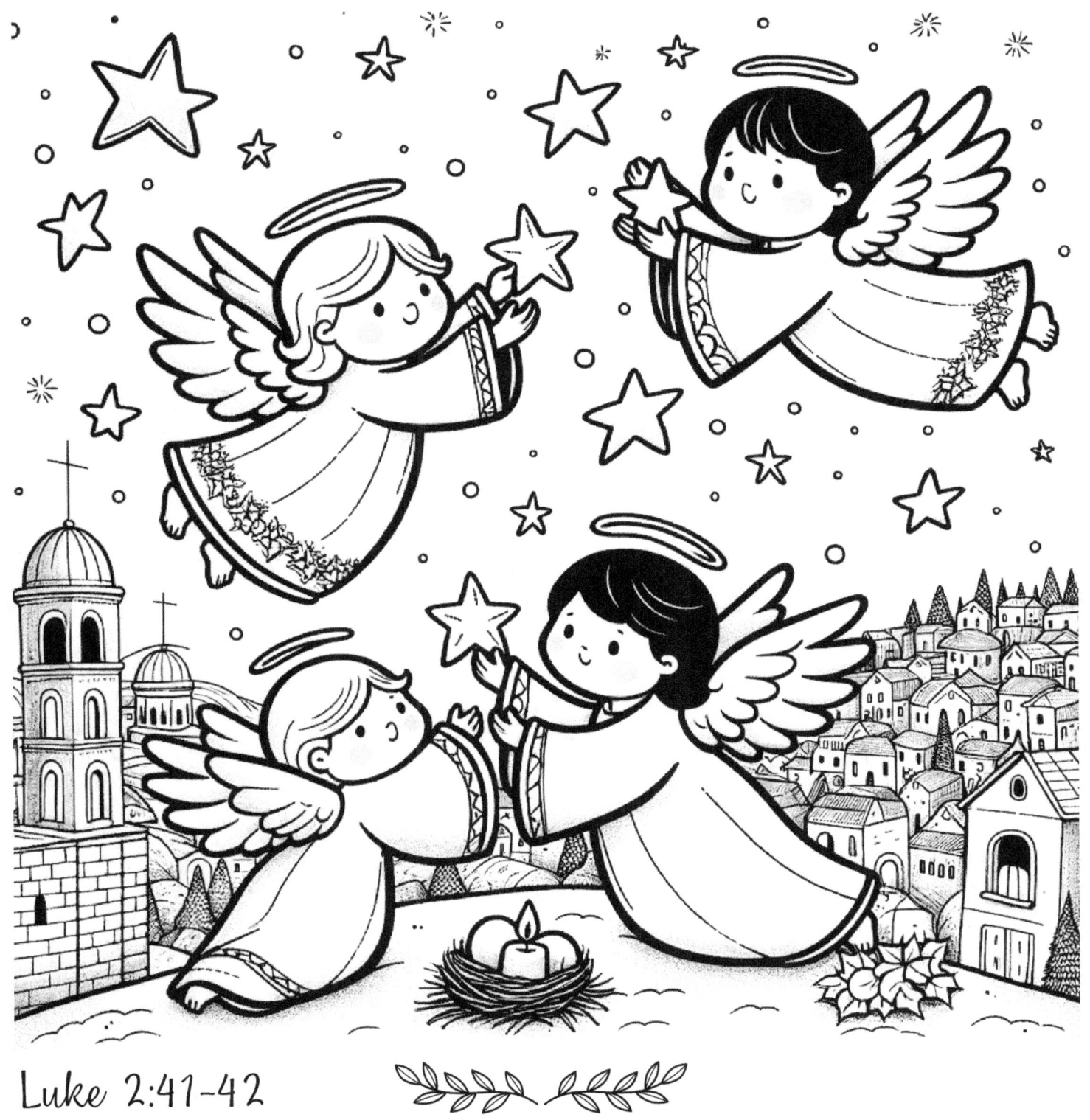

Luke 2:41-42

Every year Jesus' parents went to Jerusalem for the Passover festival. When Jesus was twelve years old, they attended the festival as usual.

ANIMALS GATHERING

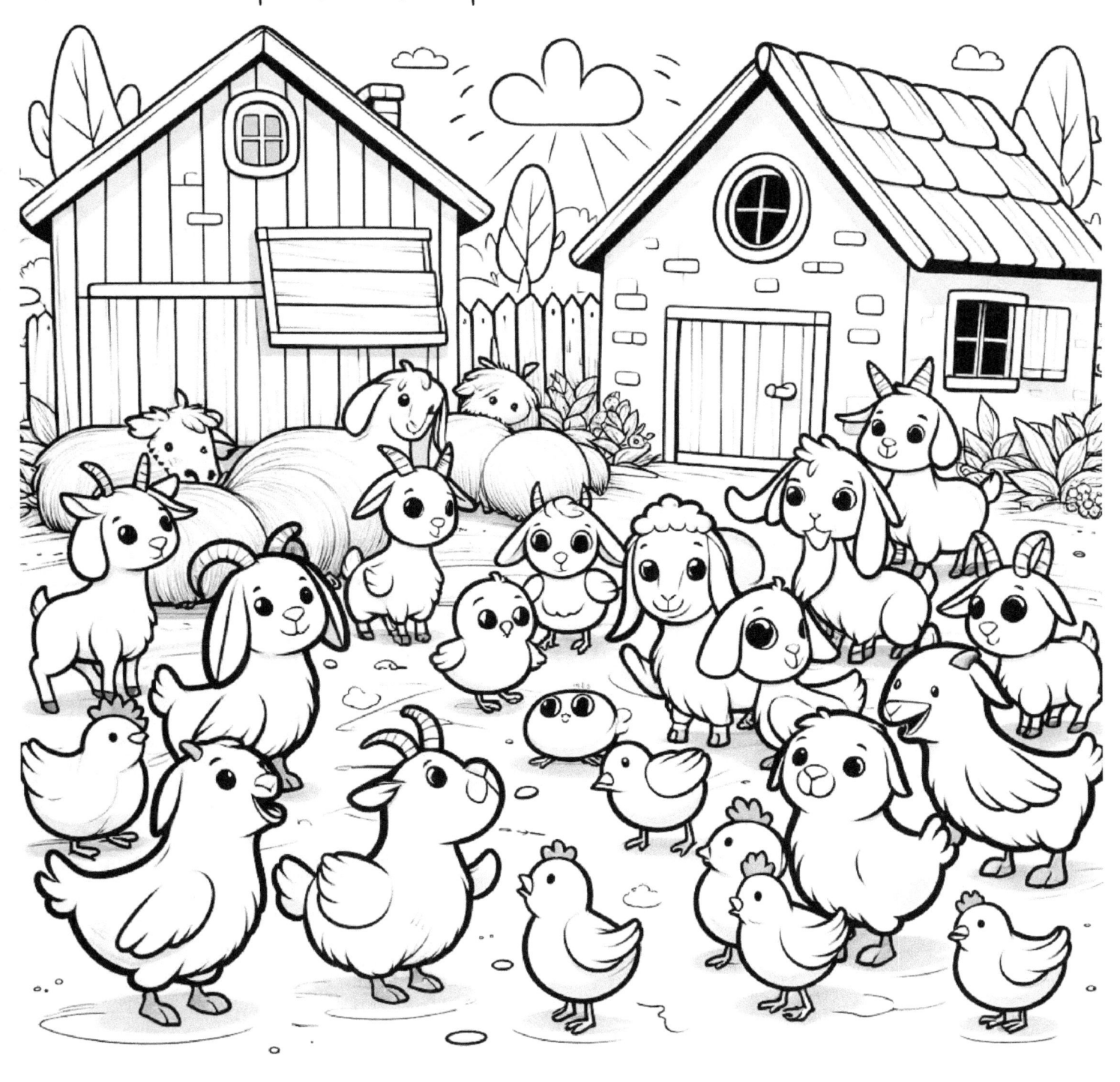

CAMPFIRE

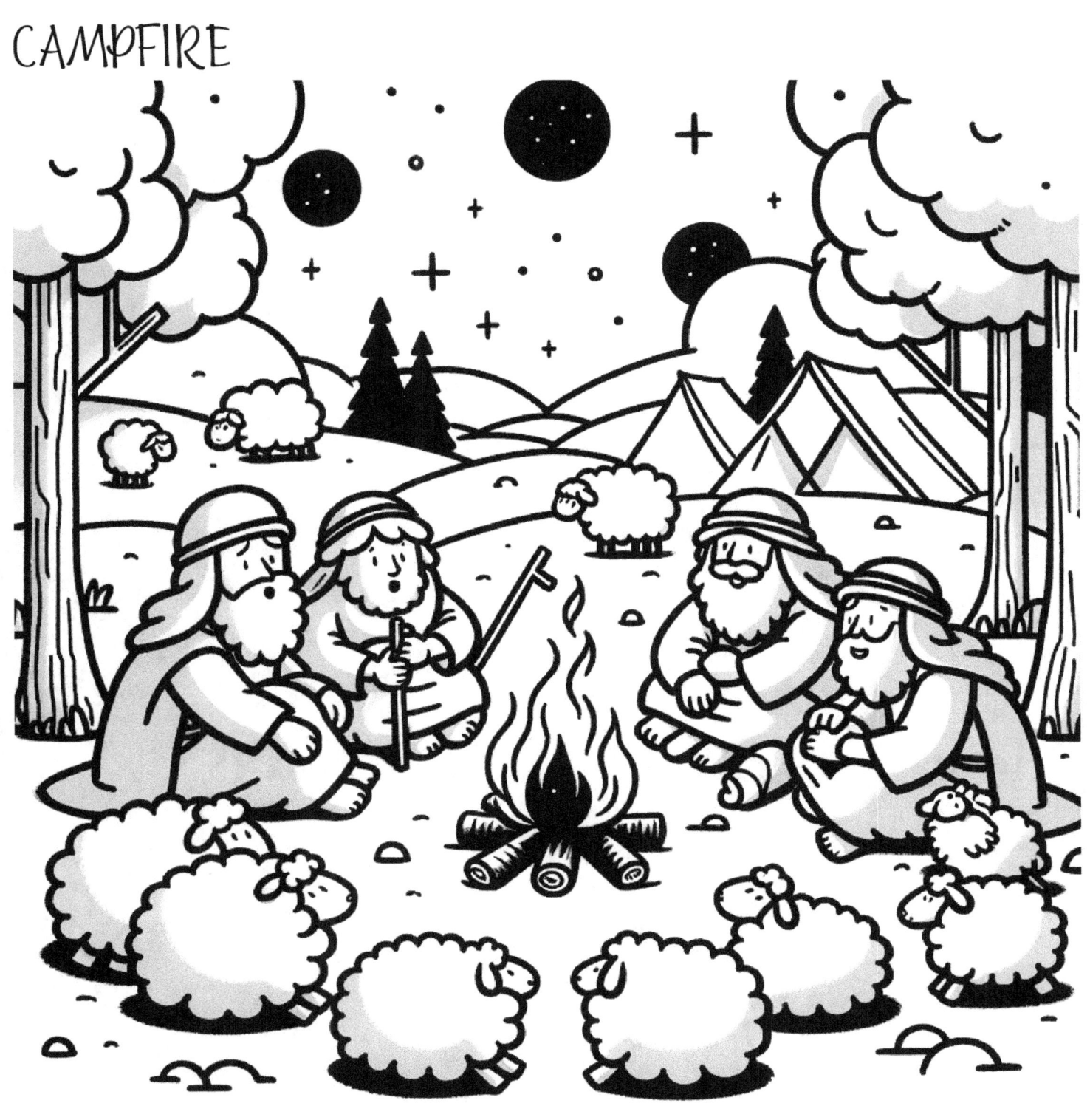

STREAM

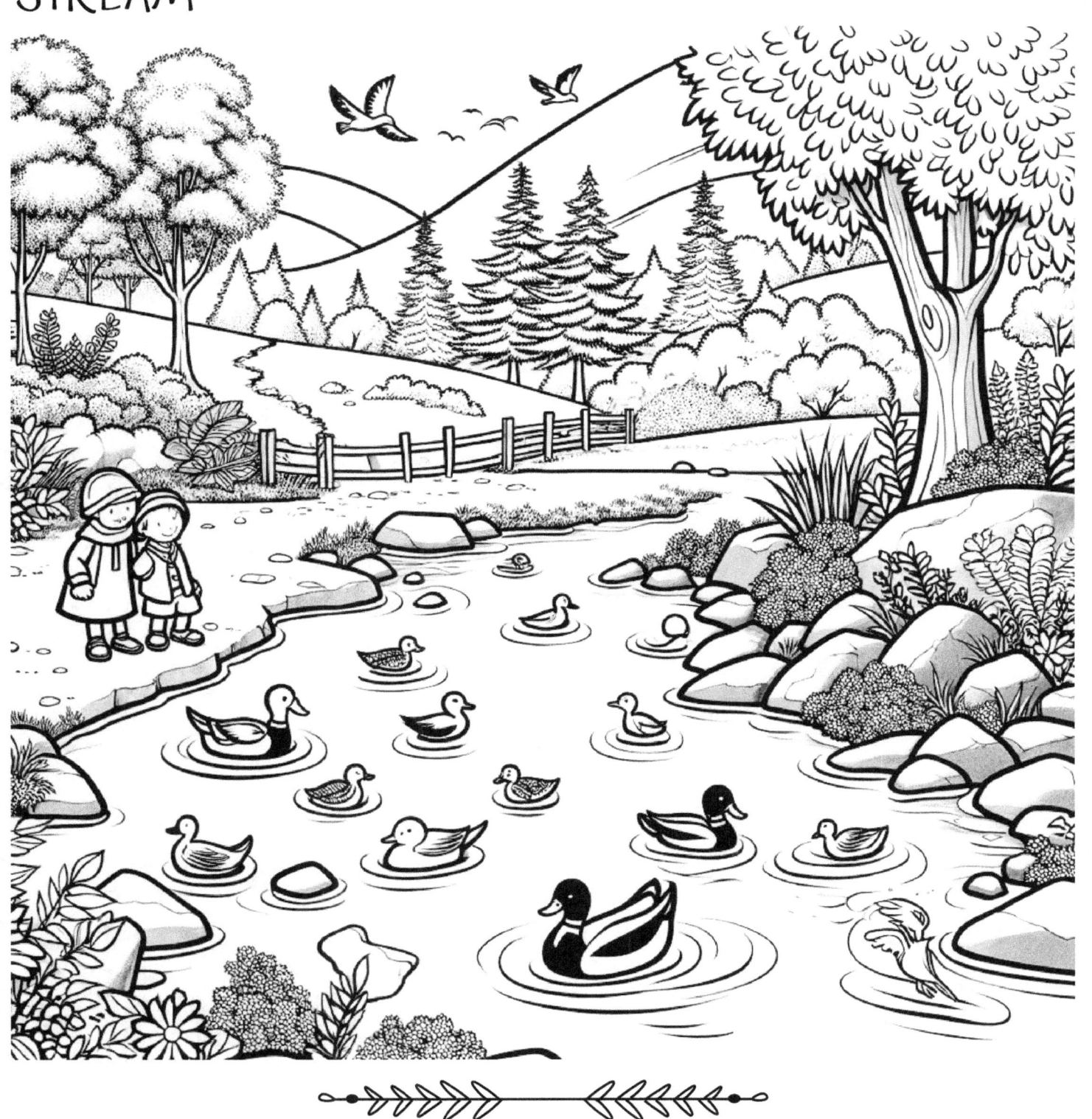

FLOWER GARDEN

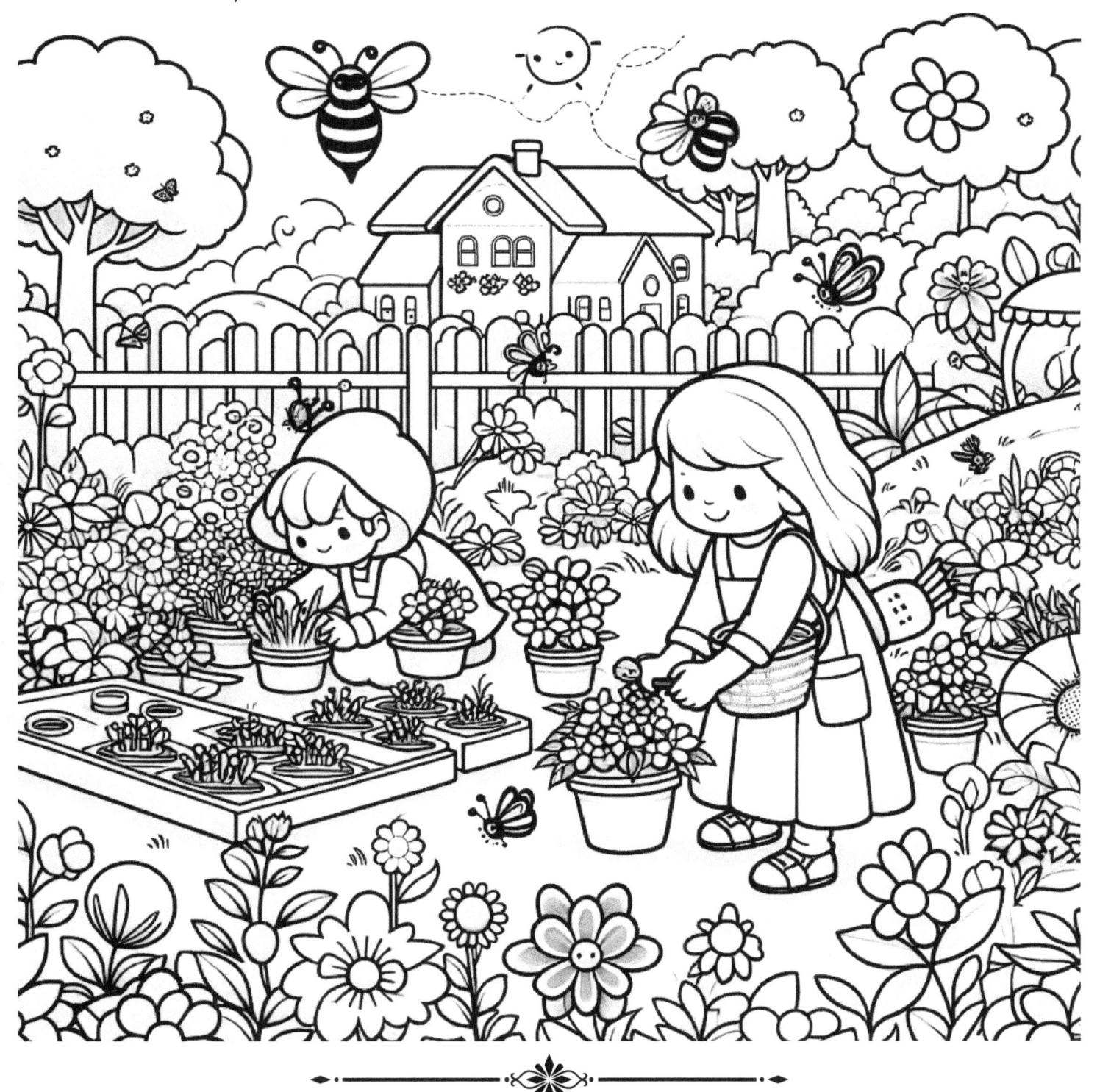

CELEBRATION

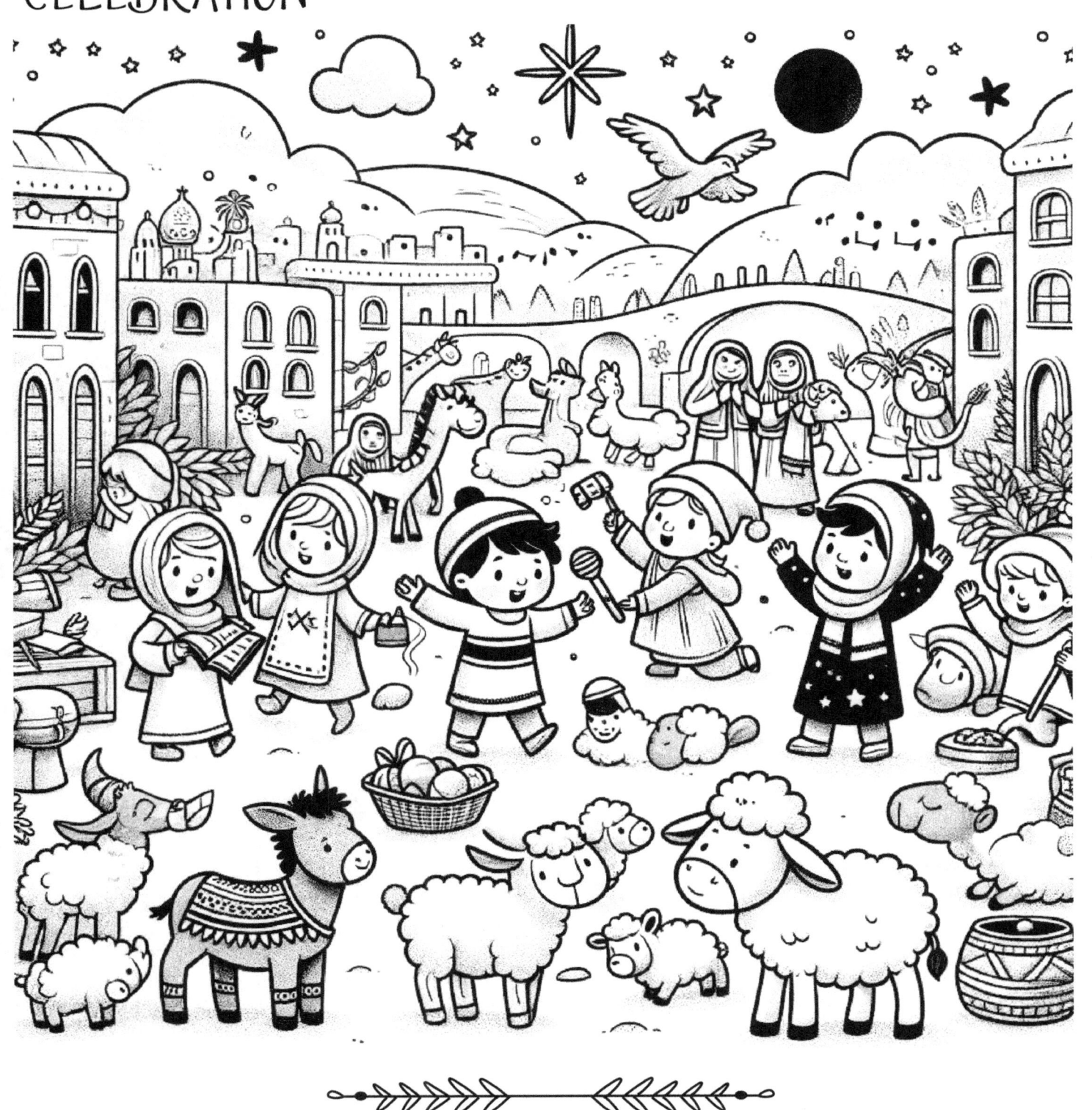

NIGHT TIME

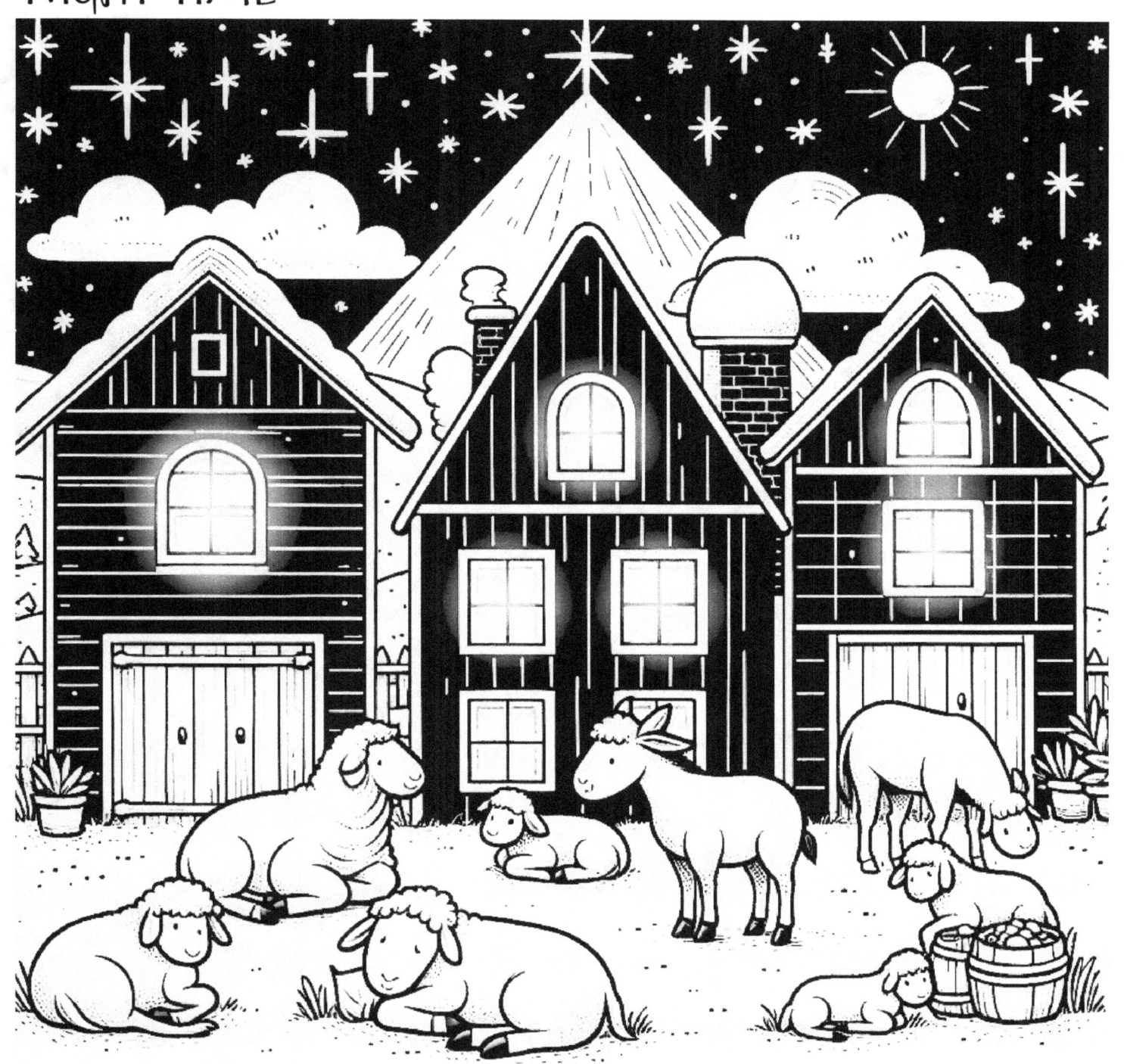

FESTIVAL

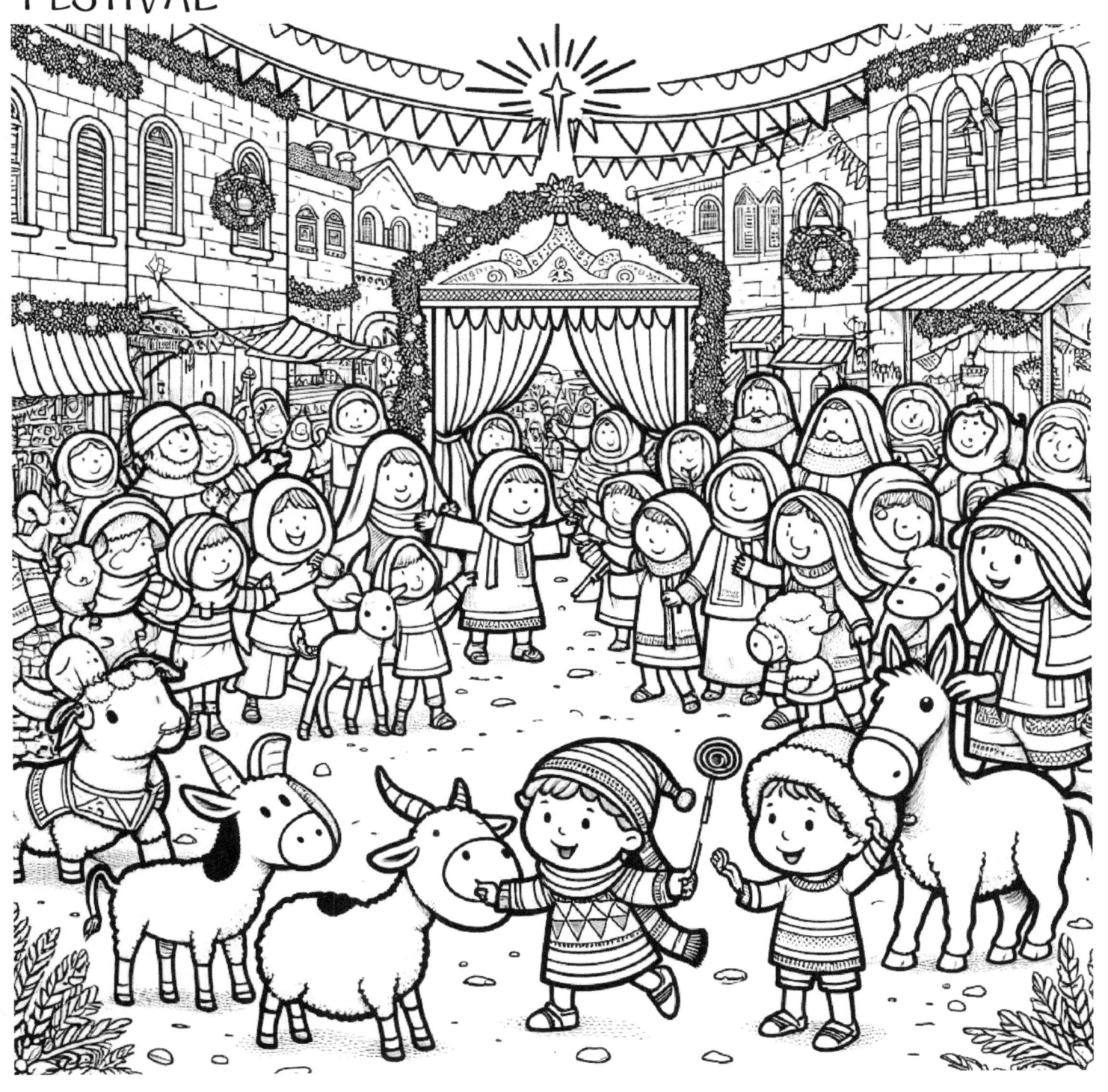

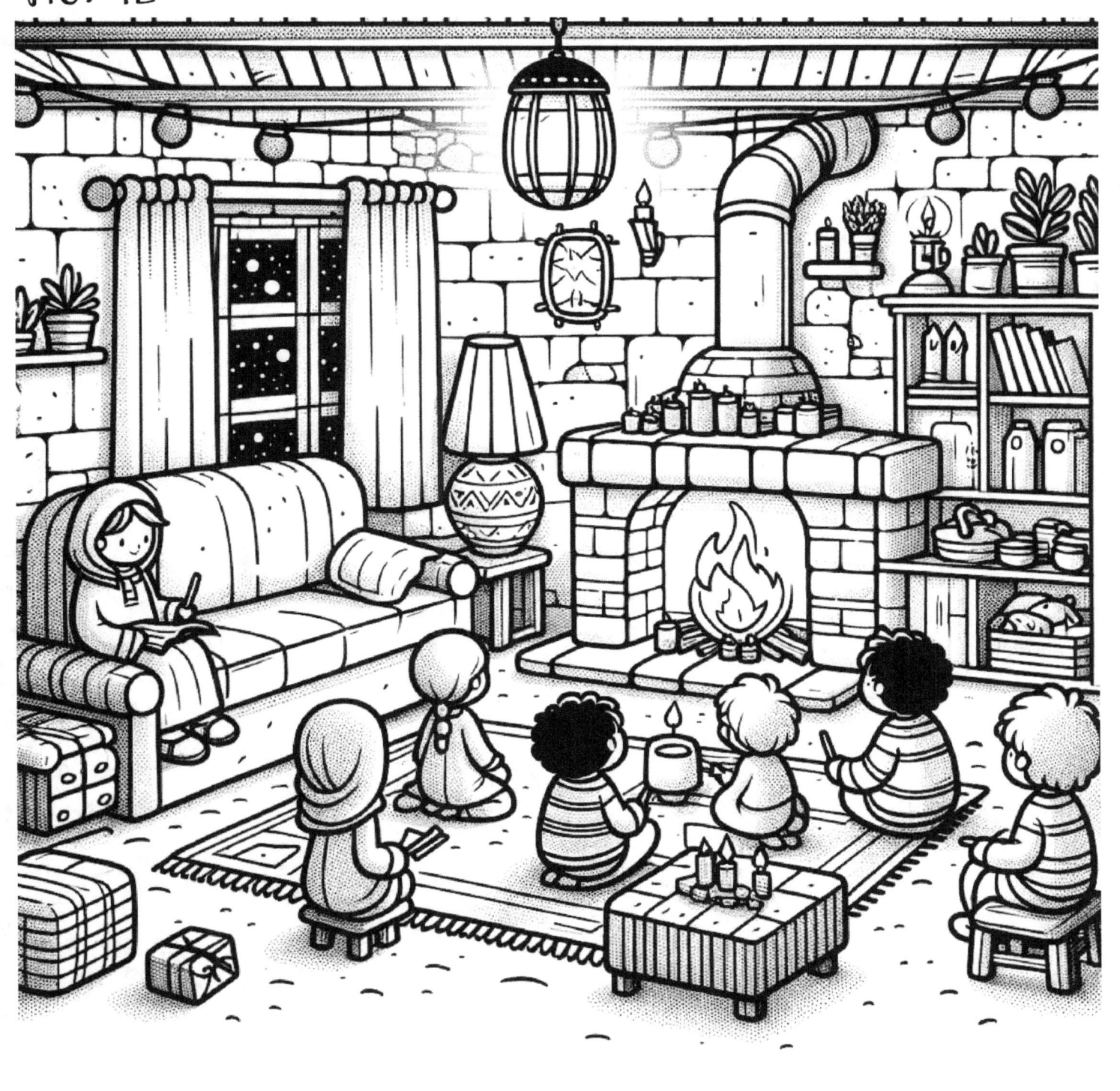

STARRY NIGHT

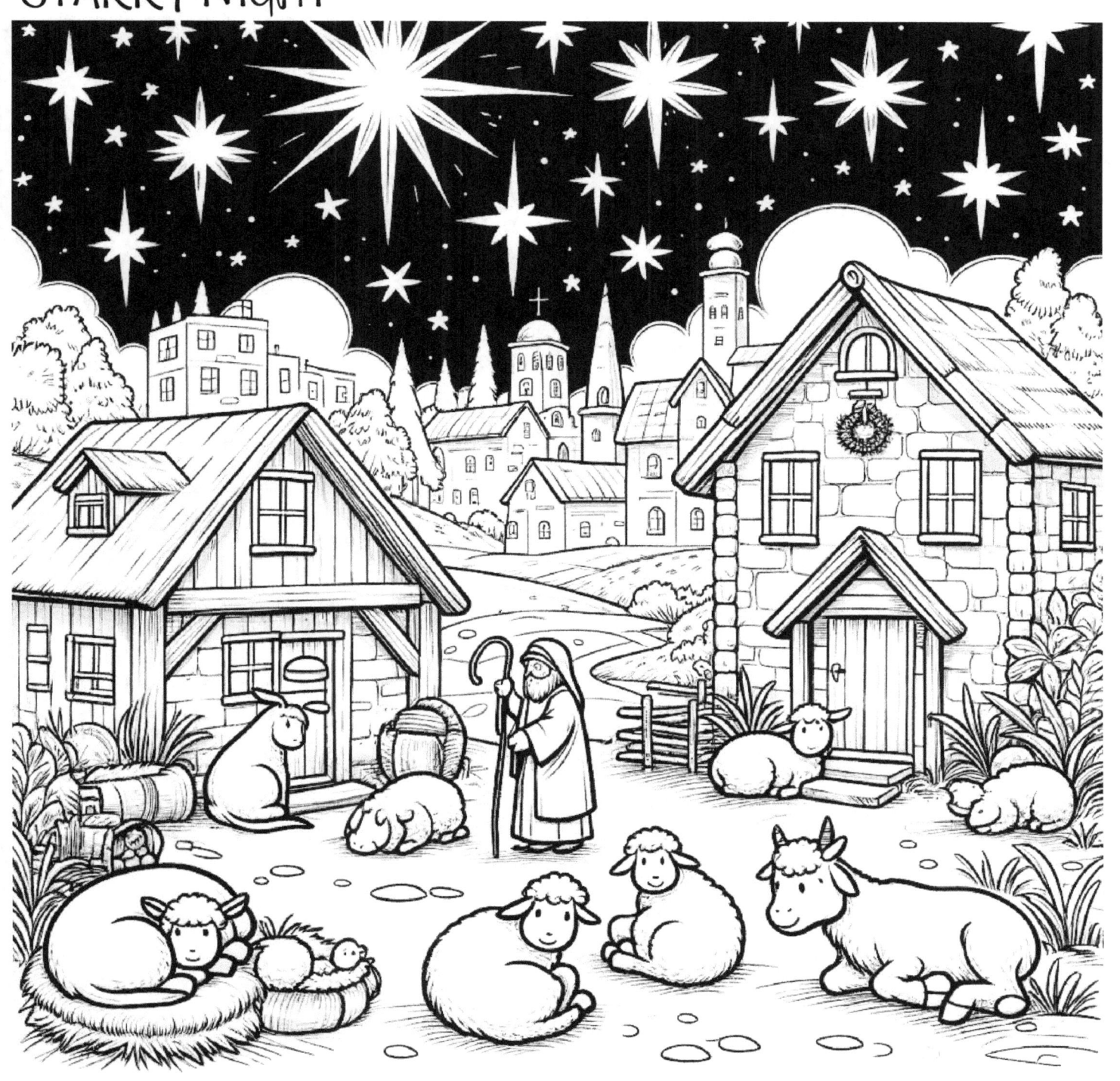